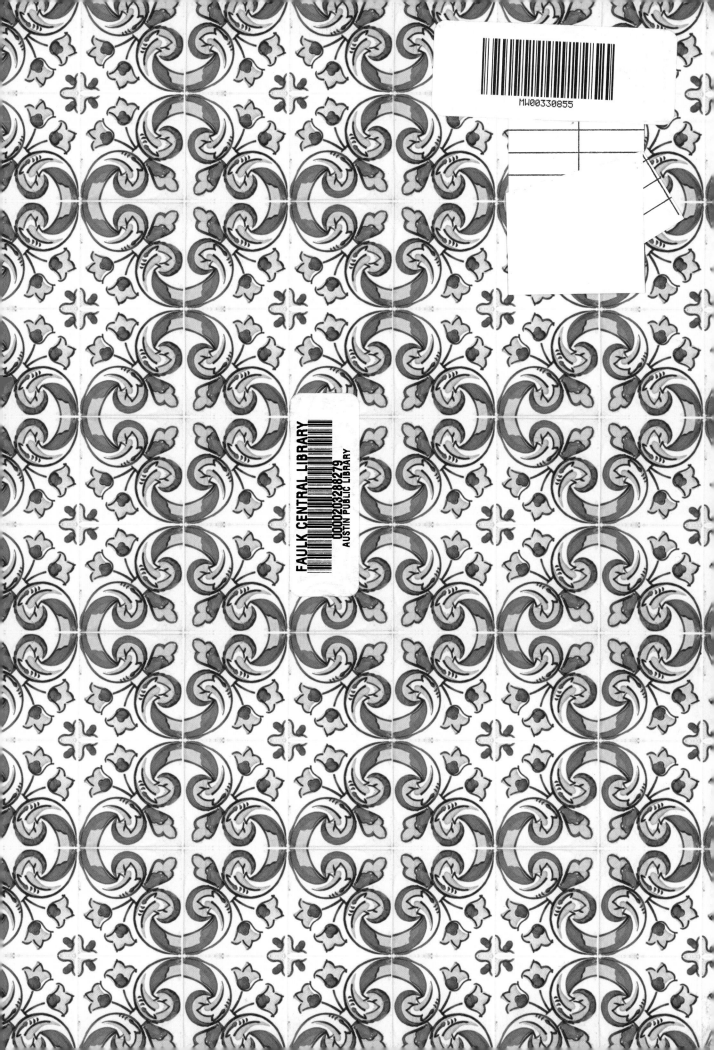

MW00330855

FAULK CENTRAL LIBRARY
0000203288279
AUSTIN PUBLIC LIBRARY

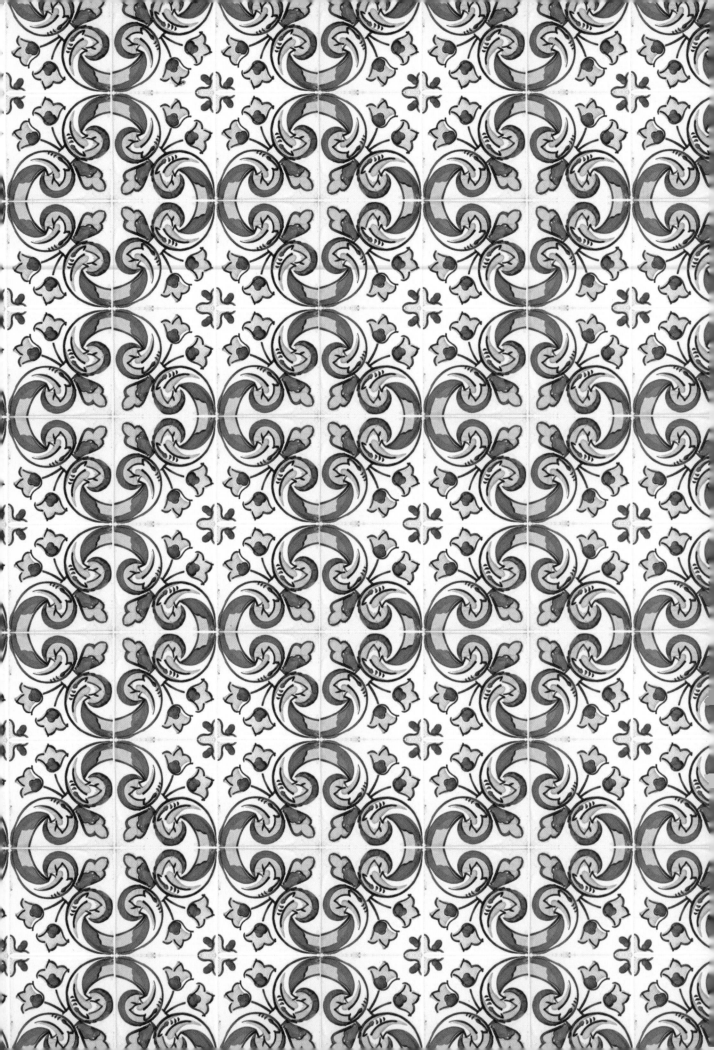

MY PORTUGAL

MY PORTUGAL
RECIPES AND STORIES

GEORGE MENDES
CHEF OF ALDEA
RESTAURANT IN
NEW YORK CITY

Genevieve Ko

PHOTOGRAPHS BY ROMULO YANES

STEWART, TABORI & CHANG
NEW YORK

TO MY MOM, FERNANDA,
MY DAD, ALEXANDRE,
AND MY SISTER, IRENE.
DEDICATED TO THE
MEMORY OF MY UNCLE
TIO ANTONIO.

POEMAS DA NOSSA ALDEIA
FERREIRÓS 22-2-77

BELO LARGO DA REPÚBLICA
O TEU NOME E UM LUARÃO
FOI DAQUI QUE CRESCEU
LINDO FERREIRÓS DO DÃO

FERREIRÓS QUANDO NASCEU
JA COM VONTADE DE TRABALHAR
FAZIA UMAS ENXADAS
PARA A TERRA DESBRAVAR

FOI BAPTIZADO DE FERREIRÓS
E LOGO COBERTO DE GLÓRIAS
FEZ A FESTA DOS MIL ANOS
ESTA GRAVADO NA HISTÓRIA

POEM BY MY GRANDFATHER HARANHO, WRITTEN TO
CELEBRATE THE HISTORY OF OUR FAMILY'S VILLAGE.

TABLE OF CONTENTS

12 INTRODUCTION

22 CHAPTER 1
SALT COD: BACALHAU

44 CHAPTER 2
THE SEA: SHELLFISH AND FISH

80 CHAPTER 3
PORK: FRESH AND CURED

106 CHAPTER 4
POULTRY: DUCK, CHICKEN, AND GAME

128 CHAPTER 5
MEAT: BEEF, VENISON, LAMB, AND GOAT

142 CHAPTER 6
SALADS, SOUPS, AND STEWS

164 CHAPTER 7
SIDE DISHES: VEGETABLES AND GRAINS

202 CHAPTER 8
DESSERTS

224 CHAPTER 9
BUILDING BLOCKS: STOCKS, SAUCES, OILS, AND SEASONINGS

248 ACKNOWLEDGMENTS

250 INDEX

INTRODUCTION

Aldea, the name of my Portuguese-inspired restaurant in New York City, means "village." And that's how intimate it felt when Portugal's President Aníbal Cavaco Silva came for lunch in 2012. Leading up to the event, I didn't think it was a big deal. As always, I focused on the food. It wasn't until my dad flew up from Florida just for the luncheon that I got it. His excitement showed me what an honor it is to cook for the leader of our native country. And it was. We had come full circle as a family: My parents left their tiny village in Portugal more than forty years earlier, and the country's leader chose to dine at the fulfillment of their son's American dream. When I was named one of *Food & Wine* magazine's Best New Chefs in 2011, I felt that I had really arrived as a chef. With the president's meal, I had come home.

And I literally went to my family's home for this book. To fully immerse myself in Portugal's regional cuisines, I drove a loop around the country, eating and drinking my way through great restaurants and taverns. And, of course, I spent a few days in Ferreirós Do Dão, my family's village in the central Beira Alta forested river region. Sharing casual home-style meals with my aunts, uncles, and cousins—many of whom I hadn't seen in years—reminded me of the honesty that I love in Portuguese cooking. The flavors are familiar to any American who's had Italian, Spanish, or Mediterranean food, with their abundant use of olive oil, onions, garlic, and herbs, but there's a distinct soulfulness to Portuguese cooking. The country is small enough to drive top to bottom in about four hours (granted, I drive fast), but that means

that land and sea come together in satisfying national dishes like pork and clams. Situated on the coastal edge of Western Europe, Portugal is the gateway to the Mediterranean and its cuisine is the epitome of light, just-caught seafood, fresh farm-to-table vegetables, and rich meat.

I consider myself lucky to have grown up with this culinary heritage, and it's the ultimate inspiration behind my cooking and career—as evident in Aldea's dishes and in this book's recipes. If there's anything I learned from my travels and my years of cooking Portuguese cuisine, it's that I've just scratched the surface of the country's culinary traditions. This book isn't a comprehensive overview or even an "authentic" representation of the cuisine. It's a collection of my personal experiences with my roots, in dishes that range from easy home-style to complex restaurant versions and in stories from my homes on both sides of the Atlantic. I didn't set out to put Portuguese cuisine on the map in America, but by refining and modernizing its simple, rustic dishes, I'm hoping to do just that at Aldea and in these pages. Even though my palate is global and my culinary style free-spirited, Portugal is at the heart of what I do.

That's probably why my dishes are deeply influenced by flavors from around the world. As the first Europeans to arrive in India, Brazil, and Japan, and the first to establish the earliest global empire in Africa, Asia, and South America, the Portuguese influenced other cuisines around the world and adapted ingredients and techniques from distant cultures into theirs. I've continued that tradition by incorporating global ingredients into my Portuguese-inspired dishes and creating new ones inspired by the former colonies.

The soul of these dishes is my celebration of pristine ingredients with creativity, focused technique, and the love of food first discovered in my Portuguese-American family. Because my family made these dishes with ingredients found in Connecticut, I know you can easily source the ingredients too. Of course, I've thrown in some of my restaurant's recipes, but even those ingredients are easy enough to get nowadays.

Portuguese home cooking is distinguished by its gutsy soulfulness, as in a warming casserole with eggs baked right into a smoky tomato and pea stew laced with savory sausage. Robust seasonings such as rustic wine marinades with smoked paprika transform basic roasts into meat saturated with mouthwatering juices and encased in crackling skin. Something as simple as caldo verde (page 153), our national collard greens soup, is just as intensely satisfying. It's a wholesome bowl of satiny pureed potato with a fresh green note from leafy collards, an underlying smoky meatiness from chouriço, and a velvety finish from fruity olive oil. It epitomizes the Portuguese balance between meat and vegetables. My restaurant cooking transforms Iberian cuisine through the context of global high-end cooking. I use the same ingredients from my home-style dishes, with the addition of seasonings from around the world, and the spirit of soulful cooking remains, albeit refined into complex, composed plates.

This is the kind of deeply satisfying food that welcomes large gatherings of family and friends. It's festive, wholesome, and so damn delicious. This book is a tour of a beautiful old country's incomparable cuisine, both rustic and refined. If you haven't already fallen for Portuguese cuisine, I hope that now you will.

You have to dig in with your hands to eat this feast of seafood at Cervejaria Ramiro, one of my favorite Lisbon restaurants.

MY STORY: IT TAKES A VILLAGE

My parents, Alexandre and Fernanda, were born and raised in Ferreirós Do Dão, a small village four hours north of Lisbon. For generations, their families lived and worked in the lush hillsides that flank the río Dão. A breathtaking stone bridge spans the water and little more than a church and soccer field line the main lane. In the surrounding woods, it's a food lover's fantasy of olive, fig, and eucalyptus trees. Each time I've returned as an adult, I'm struck by the beauty of the land and the quality of the fruits, vegetables, pigs, chickens, and goats grown and raised on it. But I knew that despite the rich natural resources, the job prospects had been bleak for my parents and life had been hard. It wasn't difficult for them to accept my aunt Natalia's invitation to join her in America. They brought with them a deep knowledge of the dishes they grew up eating and plans to keep grilling sardines and roasting suckling pig in Danbury, Connecticut, where their extended family and other villagers had immigrated en masse.

In 1969, my mom moved to Danbury. My dad came the following year, they married, and I was born four years later into a tight-knit Portuguese-American community. My aunt's restaurant was a hub for all the factory workers, my parents included, who refueled after long days on her killer bitoque steak with fried eggs. On weekends and saints' days, we all gathered at the Portuguese Club for the live band, dancing, and, of course, the food. Huge stockpots of caldo verde, the iconic collard green soup, and giant pans of pork and clams, a hearty marriage of farmland and ocean, fed the kids between foosball games and the grown-ups between rounds of beer. Sometimes, I followed my mom into that commercial kitchen. On the burners, potatoes fried in olive oil until they got really brown and crisp, making the air heavy and the floor slippery. I remember being amazed by the drama of it all and attracted to the intensity of the fierce heat.

What I remember even more clearly are the smells and tastes of home—the comfort of our daily family meals and our holiday feasts shared with more than thirty aunts, uncles, and cousins. My school mornings began at my babysitter Fernanda's home, where my mom dropped me and my sister, Irene, off on her way to the early shift at the pencil factory. For breakfast, my babysitter buttered classic Portuguese rolls and toasted them in the oven until they were crusty on the outside and soft inside. My mom and I bought the rolls on the weekends from the local bakery. She'd time it so that we'd get them the second they came out of the oven; I was addicted to that enveloping yeasty scent. My babysitter recreated that smell for me—and one-upped it with the butter—every morning. I ate her rolls hot, backpack on in her warm kitchen. To this day, I can't think of anything better than really good warm bread and butter.

Like that simple, satisfying morning ritual, the family dinners I enjoyed growing up are the reason I love food. Both my parents are very good cooks and whoever got home first or was still home before the late shift made dinner. No matter who was at the stove, I picked up the scent of refogado, the Portuguese version of soffritto, in which onions, garlic, red chile flakes, paprika, and bay leaves bubble—but never brown—in a shallow pool of olive oil until tender and golden. It's the basis of nearly everything we ate. My mom used it to start tomato rice, a savory-sweet cross between risotto and pilaf, and my dad cooked it into his garlicky shrimp, which became the inspiration for Aldea's signature shrimp alhinho. On Sundays, I could smell quail marinating in white wine, parsley, paprika, and olive oil, ready to get charred on the grill.

Our weeknight meals were great; our holiday feasts were phenomenal. My parents and their siblings had a better life in America, but there was always a longing to go back home to Portugal. And that's exactly how our Christmas meals felt. My mom and her sisters had clipped American recipes from magazines and prepared shrimp cocktail and a surf-and-turf combo of filet mignon and lobster tails, along with a side of baked potatoes topped with stewed white button mushrooms. But they also spent days making favorites from home, like caldeirada—our version of bouillabaisse—and rabbit rice. We kept the Christmas tradition of frying filhozes (sugary pumpkin doughnuts) for dessert and my uncle Anibal always made rice pudding, decorating the top by sprinkling ground cinnamon in the shapes of flowers. We'd set up long tables and folding chairs in the wood-paneled basement, placing all these dishes down the center in a casual family-style buffet, with a jug of wine on one end, kids' table on the other. At that crowded table, there was always a sense of warmth and laughter and comfort. Those meals instilled in me what food does to a crowd: It turns nourishment into real happiness. I try to do the same now at my restaurant by serving dishes so warming that the diners feel not only satiated but truly happy too.

But those meals didn't make me a chef. Honestly, I didn't fully appreciate how unique my childhood food experiences were until I began cooking professionally.

I didn't know that other people's uncles don't cure their own chouriço and linguiça in the garage. Or that other kids didn't get to stomp on grapes—barefoot and in their underwear—to make wine. I assumed everyone grew extensive vegetable and herb gardens along their driveways and that trips to the Long Island Sound were meant for collecting briny mussels. My parents, aunts, and uncles—strong cooks all—learned how to do those things on their farm back in Ferreirós Do Dão and they just kept doing them when they got to Connecticut. I didn't cook growing up, but I experienced firsthand the importance of respecting ingredients and of treating them simply to make them really satisfying. More than anything, I learned what good food is.

My grandfather, seated on the right, visited during one of our big holiday feasts.

JUST COOK

started cooking late relative to the European guys, who begin apprenticing as young as fourteen. Fourteen years old, and they've already found their calling. Me? At that age, I was attending a vocational high school, preparing for an architecture career. But I couldn't sit still for all that drafting, so I transferred to a "regular" high school when my family moved from a Portuguese enclave in Danbury, Connecticut, to Bethel, a slightly leafier suburb. My senior year, still pretty much clueless about the rest of the world and my place in it, I ended up on a field trip to the Culinary Institute of America in Hyde Park, New York.

Honestly, I don't remember too much about that trip. My strongest impression was of the students and how they looked so damn professional in their starched chefs' whites. But I was intrigued, so I banged out a four-hundred word essay on why I wanted to cook. I'll admit it was one of the most exciting days of my life, the day I was accepted.

Next came the hard part—convincing my father to let me go. Not that my dad was entirely unfamiliar with the food business. He had bussed tables at restaurants in Portugal, so he knew what a grind that life can be. He also knew that my very first job, at Ricky's Cheesesteaks (in the mall, of course), hadn't ended so well. After three weeks behind the griddle, I was ready to call it quits. So my dad phoned my manager for me and told him I had a headache and couldn't come back to work—ever again.

So I was fighting an uphill battle. Maybe that's why I did something that surprises me even now. I wrote my dad a letter. Maybe it was the shock of receiving it, or the realization his aimless teenage son had finally found his calling. Not only did my dad agree to let me

go—he also helped me fulfill one of the school's prerequisites by getting me a job in his factory's kitchen. He even drove me up to school after I completed that requirement. When I arrived on campus, I didn't even have the basic coordination needed to function in the kitchen. My nickname: "George Burns." Every day I was in the shits. I got my ass kicked, but I handled the pressure and picked up some discipline, speed, and organization along the way. While there, I studied all the French classics, which still influence dishes I create today.

To build on that repertoire, I did an externship at the Stonehenge Inn in Ridgefield, Connecticut. We tournéed all the carrots, turnips, and zucchini. Classic French. And the chef didn't let anything slide. When he caught sight of some pineapple core in a fruit salad I made, he screamed, "The only way that can be eaten is if you're a goat!" Before I could finish saying, "Sorry, chef," he screamed again to pick out every piece of pineapple. That was my first lesson in restaurant refinement.

The second was a lesson in more modern French cuisine. My teacher this time was Chef Ed Brown of Tropica in New York City, who offered me a position butchering fish in his restaurant. At that point, I had to make a decision. I had to choose whether I wanted to give up my life in suburban Connecticut to become a cook in New York City.

While at the Culinary Institute, I had visited home nearly every weekend. And during my externship, I moved back in with my parents. This wasn't unusual in our tight-knit immigrant community. All of my cousins and friends stayed close to home, getting factory jobs like our parents' or working in small local businesses. My family and community were my anchors in life: our nightly dinners, Sunday suppers after mass and soccer, birthday parties, holiday feasts. I knew that if I went to New York City to start cooking, I'd have to give all of that up.

I did.

That decision to leave home was the turning point in my career. Once I crossed that threshold, I pushed myself hard to succeed. At Tropica, I learned the invaluable skill of fish butchery and developed the techniques that prepared me for staging (basically being an unpaid apprentice) at David Bouley's original restaurant. That was a totally different level of cooking. To land a job there, I spent a whole day putting together his amuse bouche: doing a tiny mince of cold cucumber and tomato for crab salad and making mini hot quiches. I was hired to be the amuse bouche guy and learned to compose the perfect little bite. At Aldea, I still share the amuse bouche station with the rest of the team. We pipe goat cheese cream into crisp beet tuiles and balance smoked trout caviar and shiso leaves over sardines on toast. In composing starters, it's all about that sort of precision and intensity of flavors.

As Bouley showed me, there's no less precision in the main courses. For the next three years, I worked six days a week, moving from garde manger (appetizers) to entremetier (vegetables) to poissonier (fish). I was with a great rat pack of cooks: Dan Barber, Kurt Gutenbrunner, Cyril Renaud, Alex Ureña. We were doing two hundred covers a night, surviving on coffee and four hours of sleep. In that time, Chef Bouley taught me how to properly season, use herbs, cook fish, and compose a plate by creating harmony and balance in flavors and textures. I wasn't yet ready to create my own food then, but now that I am, I can see Bouley's influence on the delicate balance I've struck in Aldea's dishes.

Bouley made me a really strong line cook. More important, he began to teach me what it took to be a chef. He could see that I was struggling with giving up life outside of the kitchen. Even after I decided to leave home and to give up a normal life of free nights and weekends and time with family and friends, I still wondered if I'd made the right decision. Bouley assured me I had. He told me, "Everything I have in my life is because of this restaurant. Put 100 percent of your life into being a chef, and a life will be created for you, too. Just cook and everything will come to you." That advice made the hard sacrifices seem easy. And it became even easier to be away from family when my dad said, "Just cook. Just do your work. Stay patient. Everything else will fall into place." It all has.

A typical prep hour at Aldea.

THE ROAD TO ALDEA

When I was eight years old, my extended family road-tripped from our village in Portugal to visit relatives in France. What I remember most from that trip wasn't some phenomenal French meal—it was a car accident. My sister and I were small enough to ride, sans seat belts, in the back of my aunt's little red Renault hatchback. When the car started skidding on the rain-soaked highway, my mom did everything she could from the front passenger seat to keep us safe. In a matter of seconds, the car hit a wet slick, went airborne, and crashed into a dirt embankment. My sister and I remained relatively unscathed, but my mom's forehead was bloodied up from hitting the windshield. (Thankfully, she healed well.)

My association of France with outright terror was strengthened when I was given the opportunity to stage with chef Alain Passard at his three-Michelin-star restaurant L'Arpège in Paris. His kitchen was astoundingly organized; there was no room for mistakes. Even basic tasks like cleaning an immense number of baby chanterelles gave me an adrenaline rush. I loved the smell of those fresh mushrooms and the Zen-like peace I felt in that repetitive swiping. That crucial kitchen lesson of consistently getting each technique right each time has stuck with me, as has the importance of treating pure, fresh ingredients with respect and care.

I was influenced deeply by seeing Chef Passard take his grandmother's cooking and add exotic ingredients like citrus powder and fresh licorice root. I hadn't yet realized that I would do something similar at Aldea—that our baby goat with charred bread emulsion dish would owe as much to Passard as to my own grandmother. The allure of cooking there drew me back for a second stage. After I overcame my initial fear, the experience was magical, peaceful, grounding. I left saying, "Wow. *This* is what I want to do for the rest of my life."

I returned to New York in 1997 to be the chef at Le Zoo, an intimate downtown bistro located where The Spotted Pig is now. The freedom to do my own dishes was great, and the customers and owners liked my vibrant modern French food, especially the fish dishes. Around town, Le Zoo became known as "Bouley on a budget." I was up to the challenge of running the kitchen, but I was twenty-four and green and still wanted to learn more. For years, I had pored over Alain Ducasse's cookbook *La Riviera d'Alain Ducasse*. Those pages had a huge impact on me, and I knew I wanted to learn from him directly.

After cooking as the executive sous chef to Sandro Gamba, Ducasse's chef at Lespinasse in Washington, D.C., I got the opportunity to stage at one of Ducasse's restaurants in France: La Bastide de Moustiers in Provence. Being there, cooking the cuisine of the sun with olive oil and garlic, brought me back to my roots. We'd pick baby zucchini, carrots, radishes, and haricots verts from the garden. Then we'd glaze them individually in butter and chicken stock and finish them with sherry vinegar and black truffles. It was homey, earthy, warming, fresh, wholesome. Those vegetables were in-your-face powerful and became the guiding light for my take on from-the-farm dishes.

The real secret to Ducasse's vegetables was that he grew them right there, at the restaurant. From him, I learned that it's essential to source the best ingredients. Of course, I can't grow my own vegetables on Seventeenth Street, so I do the next best thing—I get to know the farmers who supply my restaurant.

More profoundly, the way Ducasse honed in on those fresh products and amplified their true, honest flavors reminded me so much of what my mom and aunt did at home. I began to see how the philosophy behind the homey food of my childhood and that of the intricate dishes of my professional career weren't worlds apart after all.

During those trips to Europe, the seed had been planted: I decided I'd open my own place someday. Back in New York, I helped Kurt Gutenbrunner open Wallsé, his downtown Austrian restaurant. Seeing my friend put his heritage out there made me want to connect further with mine.

To bridge the gap between the Iberian cuisine of my childhood and my formal training since, I staged with avant-garde Basque chef Martin Berasategui at his three-Michelin-star restaurant in San Sebastian, Spain. Berasategui was riding the wave of refining Spanish cuisine with his personal interpretations of traditional dishes. No matter how far he pushed the envelope with new techniques, he always stayed true to the ingredients' inherent flavors. A prime example: He created little pillows of translucent sheets of cuttlefish filled with squid ink sauce. When it burst in your mouth, you were hit with the very essence of cuttlefish and squid and a real taste of the Basque region.

After my stage in Spain, I returned to New York City and became chef de cuisine at Tocqueville, where I worked with the Brazilian-born chef Marco Moreira. My Tocqueville dishes fused classic and modern French with the Mediterranean flavors of Ducasse and the avant-garde techniques of Berasategui. All the while, trying to remain true to my roots, I started adding touches of luxury to rustic Portuguese dishes. As a play on my mom's rice dishes, I seared shrimp and foie gras to serve over saffron rice. I started curing my own bacalhau and refining traditional applications.

While at Tocqueville, I finally scored a reservation at Ferran Adrià's El Bulli in Spain (after fifty emails and a dozen faxes). That meal totally blew my mind. As magical and technically innovative as the food was, it was still delicious. That's the key to any great meal. If the food isn't delicious, everything else is irrelevant. That night, I began trying to stage there.

What began as an inspirational meal turned into a stage that gave me the confidence to create the dishes for Aldea. At El Bulli, they gave me a "tour," letting me work practically every station in the course of two weeks. At every station, Adrià routinely took second- and third-place ingredients and made them the stars. He treated sardines with as much care as lobsters. In a pine nut and foie gras dish, he made the pine nuts shine. In other cases, he took those humble ingredients alone and elevated them, such as a dish of just asparagus or just peanuts.

Working with Adrià, I began to reflect on the style I was cultivating. That time—and the years of experience before it—gave me not only the confidence to create from within and to trust my palate, but to know traditional flavors too. Passard's reinterpretation of his grandmother's cooking, Ducasse's Mediterranean simplicity, Berasategui's and Adrià's avant-garde Spanish innovations: They were all taps on my shoulder saying, "Hey, remember your childhood?" But it was Adrià who, by example, showed me that I could showcase Portuguese cuisine without being confined to it. El Bulli was ostensibly "Spanish," but there were at least five courses at any one time that were definitely Japanese. It was freeing to realize that there was no reason I couldn't do other dishes too. I'm a free-spirited chef, spontaneous and passionate and unwilling to be defined by one genre. Honestly, I'd get bored sticking to one cuisine. I realized then that Portugal touches everything I do—and I wanted to do everything. I was ready.

I left Tocqueville hungry for more. There are huge risks in opening a restaurant, but I knew what I wanted. The food: Portuguese-inspired global with the utmost respect for seasonality. The vibe: modern and fun, a casual restaurant with high-end food. While constructing the space for the restaurant, I kept cooking. Every spare moment, I jotted food notes on my phone and sketched dishes in notepads. Then I tried them out at charity events and dinner parties.

Aldea started with the vibrant energy of what I put on the plate: simple, classic, modern, clean flavors; striking, precise presentation; above all, authenticity. Yes, I wanted to honor traditional Portuguese food, but I was also committed to being true to myself in creating a dish. I sometimes had to stop myself from touching a dish that was already good. The worst thing I could do was ruin the ingredients.

That's where my dishes start. It's what every mentor taught me along the way: Get the very best ingredients and make them better. That mantra is as true for my home-style classic Portuguese dishes as for my restaurant ones. After finding and developing a harmony and balance of flavors, I refine the presentation. When I think I'm done, I always ask myself,

"Is this delicious? Does it make me feel nourished?" I consider the multileveled flavors and textures, and whether I need something more. When I first served my arroz de pato to my partners, I looked at the plates going out and realized, "I forgot the duck skin cracklins!" I chased the plates and spooned the cracklins on tableside. That savory crunch makes the dish.

My recipes started turning into my menu, which I wanted to be tight and focused. At Aldea, we did refined takes on Portuguese classics, such as putting bacalhau à bras, classically simple scrambled eggs with salt cod, into cut egg shells and using a charged siphon to pipe in a salt cod cream, and cooking shrimp heads to create an intense jus for garlic-seared shrimp. My time cooking in the Mediterranean turned into a summery dish of green beans with peaches and almonds. Portugal's seafaring past transformed into cuttlefish coconut curry. Adrià's brilliant combinations of sea and land inspired me to reinterpret the classic Portuguese combination of pork and clams.

Aldea's first menu combined simple plates and complex ones; some dishes were hearty and rustic, others clean and light. That's what keeps food interesting. Aldea's range of dishes—and the recipes in this book—define who I am as a chef. The restaurant itself is also a reflection of my food philosophy. It's a stone's throw from the Union Square Greenmarket, where local farms sell seasonal produce. The ambience of Aldea's interior mirrors the food—modern and sleek with glass and steel, rustic and raw with exposed concrete, warm and nurturing with live birch trees. But it's the people at Aldea who make the restaurant what it is. Every sous chef, line cook, manager, server, busser, dishwasher, bartender, hostess, and, of course, diner who's been with us has become family.

CHAPTER 1

SALT COD: BACALHAU

LEARNING TO LOVE SALT COD

2002 | OUREM, PORTUGAL

Walk into the back of a Portuguese market and you'll be hit with the fishiness you might smell at a pier. That's just one of the reasons I didn't like salt cod as a kid. At most of these markets, the dried cod comes in cardboard-stiff planks, which need to be repeatedly soaked in water and drained to rid the fish of its saltiness. At its best, bacalhau has an incomparable fresh sea flavor and silky texture and is incredibly versatile in the kitchen, as evidenced by the many ways it's used in Portuguese cooking. On my last trip to Lisbon, I actually picked up a cookbook with more than one thousand bacalhau recipes.

Starting in the sixteenth century, Portuguese fishermen began catching cod off the Newfoundland coast and preserving it by salting the fish at sea. Nowadays, most of the bacalhau in Portugal—and America—comes from Norway and Iceland. My family, like every other Portuguese family in the world, cooks with it all the time. But, honestly, I hated it when I was young. I didn't like the smell, and I imagine most people who haven't tried it before might feel the same way.

My early aversion is the reason I can say that I'm sure you'll like bacalhau if you have a great version of it. I didn't have that revelation until I was an adult well into my cooking career. Between my gigs as a chef in New York, my dad took me on a vacation to Portugal. In Ourem, he sought out his favorite restaurant, O Curral, which translates literally to "pig sty." Outside was a wood-burning grill where the matron of the place cooked the highest-quality bacalhau and simply drizzled it with fruity local olive oil. The charred fish came with collard greens and potatoes doused in that same oil. For the first time in my life, I fell in love with bacalhau. It was meaty, slightly salty, and smoky. I began imagining all I could do with this Portuguese staple . . . starting with making it myself.

The version at O Curral still retained the natural sweetness and delicate flakiness of mild fresh cod, but had that extra depth of flavor from being preserved. Just-caught cod actually verges on being bland and tastes better when salted, but the supermarket varieties I grew up eating were dried to a leathery state that I felt didn't do it any favors. When I thought about how I could recreate O Curral's version, I realized that I could simply salt fresh cod myself. All I needed was cod and salt and a fridge. The early Portuguese explorers didn't have that last modern luxury, but it's made a world of difference in my bacalhau dishes.

Now, I can keep the moisture in the cod by salting it just enough to infuse it with flavor and transform its texture from fall-apart flaky to silky with just the right chew. I still soak the cured cod in cold water to rid it of excess salt. (This step is crucial because you don't actually want salt cod to be too salty.) It may be counterintuitive to take the smart idea my ancestors had of salt-preserving to semi-preserving that same fish, but I think of it as progress. Try my version of bacalhau and you'll taste exactly what I mean.

SALT COD AND POTATO CROQUETTES

BASIC SALT COD

BACALHAU

By curing cod yourself, you get the delicate sweetness of the fish under an intense savory richness and smooth-as-butter texture. It requires only two ingredients and a little patience and planning. Do it: It's a revelation.

MAKES ABOUT 3 POUNDS (1.4 KG)

kosher salt 1½ pounds (680 g)
whole skin-on cod fillet 4¼ pounds (1.9 kg),
1½ inches (4 cm) thick, bones removed

Four days before serving, spread ½ inch (12 mm) of the salt in a 6-inch- (15-cm-) deep container. Place the cod on top, skin-side down, and cover it with the remaining salt, patting it against the top and sides of the fish. Cover tightly with plastic wrap and refrigerate for 48 hours. Occasionally tip out excess moisture that's been released and evenly distribute the salt around the cod again.

Rinse the cod under cold running water, then rinse out the container. Return the cod to the container and cover it with cold water. Cover tightly with plastic wrap and refrigerate for 2 to 3 days, changing the water every 16 hours. Because the saltiness of the fish can vary, I start tasting it after 2 days. I want a slight salinity and will drain the cod when it's where I want it. Remember that you'll be using the cod in other dishes that you'll season again, so you don't want it to be too salty. Drain the cod well and use immediately.

HANG DRY

To make the bacalhau even more flavorful, I've started wrapping the salt-covered fish in cheesecloth and hanging it in the walk-in refrigerator. The technique on page 26 works well and is totally foolproof, but the liquid the fish sits in as a result of the curing can slightly dilute the flavor. This trick keeps the cod dry. Keep in mind that it also makes it slightly more salty.

All you have to do is cut two pieces of cheesecloth 8 inches (20 cm) longer than the length of the fish and three times as wide. Stack the two pieces, then spread ½ inch (12 mm) salt the size of the fish in the center. Place the cod on top, skin-side down, and cover it with the remaining salt, patting it against the top and sides of the fish. If you plan to hang the fish, fold in the long sides of cheesecloth, overlapping them in the center. If not, fold in the short sides of cheesecloth tightly against the fish, then the long sides, overlapping the pieces. Tie the fish very tightly in the center with kitchen string, forming a cylinder. Repeat tying at 5-inch (12-cm) intervals, keeping the cylinder shape and tying as tightly as possible. If you're hanging it, twist the ends, then tie them very tightly with a long piece of kitchen string.

Hang the fish so that the thin tail is on top and the thick end is on the bottom. Place a dish underneath to catch any drips. If you are not hanging it, place the fish on a wire rack set in a sheet pan or roasting pan.

Refrigerate for 3 days and unwrap. If you're not ready to use the cod right away, brush off the salt and refrigerate it on a wire rack set in a sheet pan for up to 2 weeks. Three days before you're ready to use the fish, rinse it under cold running water. Place the cod in a large container and cover it with cold water. Cover tightly with plastic wrap and refrigerate for 3 days, changing the water twice a day. (As I mention on page 26, the soaking time may vary. Start tasting the cod after 3 days and drain it when it's just slightly salty.) Drain the cod well and use immediately.

SALT COD AND POTATO CROQUETTES

Idaho potatoes	1 pound (455 g), scrubbed well
kosher salt	to taste
Basic Salt Cod (page 26)	1 pound (455 g)
fresh parsley leaves	2 tablespoons, very finely chopped
extra-virgin olive oil	1 tablespoon plus 1 teaspoon
fresh lemon juice	1¼ teaspoons, plus wedges for serving
eggs	2 large, beaten
canola oil	for frying
Maldon sea salt	for serving

BOLOS DE BACALHAU

In America, we tend to think of croquettes as hot-out-of-the-oil crunchy. But this classic Portuguese snack is savory enough to be served at room temperature, with its golden shell lightly crisp. My mom used to make batches of these for the holidays early in the morning so she wouldn't be slaving over the pot once guests arrived. You can do the same.

SERVES 12

SPECIAL EQUIPMENT:
> FOOD MILL OR RICER

Put the potatoes in a saucepan just big enough to fit them in one layer. Add enough cold water to cover them by 2 inches (5 cm) and dissolve enough kosher salt in the liquid to make it taste like the ocean. Bring to a boil over high heat, then lower the heat to simmer until the potatoes are fork-tender, about 1 hour. With a slotted spoon, transfer the potatoes to a bowl and let cool, reserving the cooking liquid.

While the potatoes cool, slip the salt cod into the reserved cooking liquid and adjust the heat so that the water's hot but not simmering. Poach the salt cod until it's opaque and flakes easily, about 3 minutes. With a slotted spoon, transfer the cod to a bowl lined with a clean kitchen towel. Gently mash into small flakes. Wrap the towel around the salt cod and squeeze out as much liquid as possible. The secret to this recipe: The cod has to be dry. So keep squeezing and discarding the liquid.

Peel the potatoes, cut into chunks, and pass through the fine setting on a food mill or a ricer into a large bowl. Fold in the dried salt cod until well combined, then fold in the parsley, olive oil, and lemon juice. Finally, fold in 1 egg. You don't want the mixture too moist; it should be firm enough to shape into quenelles (football shapes). This is a simple recipe, but the croquettes will just fall apart if the mixture's too wet. Fold in the remaining egg, a little at a time, until you get a creamy, not soupy, consistency. Season to taste with kosher salt.

Fill a small saucepan with canola oil to a depth of 2 inches (5 cm). Bring it to 335°F (170°C) over medium-high heat. Use two soup spoons to form the cod mixture into quenelles and carefully lower them into the oil. Don't crowd the pan; fry a few at a time. Fry, adjust-ing the heat to maintain the temperature and turning the quenelles occasionally to evenly brown, until golden and hot throughout, about 6 minutes. Drain on paper towels. Repeat with the remaining mixture.

Sprinkle with the Maldon salt and serve with the lemon wedges.

CRUISING CASCAIS

2013 | CASCAIS

One of the great things about championing Portuguese cuisine in America is meeting others who do the same. Rui Abecassis, an owner of the Portuguese wine importing company Obrigado Vinhos, walked into Aldea more than five years ago to sell me on his wines and has since become a close friend. With his tortoise-shell glasses and well-pressed Oxford shirts, he looks like a stylish professor and he carries himself with the international-jet-set air that comes with being the son of diplomats and spending his career in New York, South America, and Europe. He now splits his time between Lisbon and Manhattan, doing as much as an ambassador for Portuguese culture as he does as a wine distributor.

I got to experience that firsthand when we decided to meet for lunch in Lisbon. Because I was just driving through, he suggested I skip the city traffic and meet him in his nearby hometown, Cascais. The only instruction he gave me was to find him at the marina. Walking along the waterfront, I passed fast food chains and I know Rui has better taste than that. He told me to keep going and I eventually found him at the dock, barefoot, clad in white shorts, with a big grin plastered on his face.

He welcomed me with "Let's go!" and gestured toward a gorgeous bayliner boat with his friends perched on the seats. Tempting as it all looked, I was on a tight schedule and told Rui I didn't have time for a ride. But he insisted, "It's Saturday! Come on! It's just lunch." Just lunch turned out to be a spin along the coast, where we could see ornate traditional buildings juxtaposed with minimalist modern glass ones. When we stopped in view of an old stone castle, Rui jumped into the bracing Atlantic. Neither Genevieve nor I came prepared, but Genevieve borrowed a suit from Rui's girlfriend and dove in along with everyone else.

As soon as they climbed back aboard, Rui started pouring a crisp, dry rosé vinho verde and passing around the bolos de bacalhau he brought for lunch. While Rui uncorked a minerally white vinho verde, I sped the boat out to rocky cliffs before turning back to shore. Cutting through the waves, smelling the salt water, and biting into the parsley-flecked cod-potato croquettes: It was a taste of true Portuguese leisure. Sure, the boat was a total luxury, but bolos de bacalhau is the kind of humble dish lots of families eat for lunch on a lazy Saturday.

I ended up running late the rest of the day, but I'm glad I took Rui up on his lunch offer. He knows the pace I keep in New York; this meal reminded me how important it is in Portuguese culture to slow down and enjoy a meal with friends. And the food doesn't have to be plated Michelin-level restaurant creations. Cod fritters on napkins with chilled wine in plastic cups can be just as good.

The coastline of Cascais.

29

FARM EGG, SALT COD, BLACK OLIVES, AND CRUNCHY POTATOES

pitted Kalamata olives	¼ cup (35 g)
whole milk	½ cup (120 ml)
Basic Salt Cod (page 26)	1 fillet (2 ounces/57g) plus 3 ounces (86 g), flaked
kosher salt and freshly ground white pepper	to taste
eggs	4 large
extra-virgin olive oil	2 tablespoons
shallot	1 small, thinly sliced
garlic clove	1, minced
fresh parsley leaves	2 tablespoons, chopped
fresh lemon juice	¼ teaspoon
Fried Shoestring Potatoes (page 194)	2 tablespoons

BACALHAU À BRÁS

Classically, this is simply served in a mound. You can do that according to the variation below or try the refined version we serve at Aldea by layering the components in an eggshell. (You need one of those cool egg cutters to make the serving cups.) Be sure to use organic, free-range eggs, preferably from a local farm. To elevate the flavors and textures, I add a creamy espuma and dehydrated olives. Subtle, refined, and as satisfying as the original.

SERVES 4

SPECIAL EQUIPMENT:
> SIPHON WITH TWO N₂O CHARGES
> EGG CUTTER

Preheat the oven to 200°F (90°C). Place the olives on a parchment-lined half sheet pan and bake until totally dried and easy to crumble. Alternatively, use a dehydrator set at 145°F (62°C). Cool completely, then mince. You should have about 2 tablespoons.

In a small saucepan, bring the milk to a simmer over medium heat. Add the salt cod fillet, remove from the heat, and let stand for 30 minutes. Pour through a fine-mesh sieve, pushing hard to strain as much liquid as possible into a clean saucepan. Reserve the cod for another use. Season the milk with salt and pepper to taste and heat to a simmer, stirring occasionally. Immediately transfer to a siphon fitted with two N₂O charges.

Use an egg cutter to carefully cut the tops off the eggs; reserve the shells and discard the tops (or see Variation). Pour the eggs into a small bowl and whisk well. Carefully peel off and discard the thin membranes inside the shells. Rinse the shells with warm water and let stand in the carton to dry.

Heat a medium nonstick pan over low heat and coat with the oil. Add the shallot and garlic and sweat, stirring occasionally, until translucent. Add the flaked cod and cook, stirring, for 15 seconds, then add the eggs and a few grindings of pepper. Cook, stirring constantly, until the eggs are just set but still wet. Fold in the parsley, lemon juice, and two-thirds of the olives and potatoes.

Use a small spoon to immediately and carefully divide the egg mixture among the four prepared eggshells. Siphon the milk mixture on top to come above the rim of the shell, then top with the remaining olives and potatoes. Serve immediately.

VARIATION

Omit the eggshell step. Siphon the salt cod milk onto serving plates and top with the egg mixture and garnishes.

PETISCOS AND BEER

When we were planning Aldea's menu, we decided to create petiscos, small snacks eaten throughout Portugal. The inevitable question from media, fellow chefs, and even my own staff was, "Are they like tapas?" The answer, "Sort of." The dishes and flavors are distinct from Spanish ones, and the type of food that counts as petiscos can range widely. In Portugal, some spots specialize in a prepared, cooked dish, such as bifana meat sandwiches or herbed snails. Other places, such as wine bars, will offer plates of cheese and charcuterie as petiscos. At Aldea, we do both.

The key to a good petisco lies in delivering a hit of flavor that simultaneously satiates your hunger and whets your appetite. Classic savory snacks, such as seasoned nuts and marinated olives, require little effort and deliver great flavor. At Aldea, we offer those, along with our take on homemade petiscos. We've taken classic Portuguese plated dishes, such as bacalhau à Brás, and miniaturized them into small bites. We've also created snacks inspired by my years of cooking globally, as with my sea urchin toast.

Even though the defining characteristics of petiscos vary, the one accompaniment that doesn't is beer. A glass of vinho verde or any nice wine is lovely with these snacks, but a good beer's what I really crave. And I'm not the only one. Throughout Portugal, you'll find our national beers—dominated by the giants Super Bock and Sagres—on tap and being poured from bottles at bars, restaurants, cafés, and stands in outdoor squares. When I toured the Museum of Beer in Lisbon, I learned that the Portuguese wine industry tried to ban beer from the country in the seventeenth century. What the winemakers viewed as a bourgeois beverage had been produced in the country for two centuries already at that point, but was starting to make inroads among wine drinkers. Over the next three centuries, the two industries came to coexist peacefully. I experienced that firsthand the same day I visited the museum. I met a group of guys, all of whom work in wine, for a drink before our wine-tasting dinner. Along with our petiscos, we all ordered beer. For all the savory, rustic flavors of Portuguese petiscos, it's exactly what I want.

FARM EGG, SALT COD, BLACK OLIVES, AND CRUNCHY POTATOES

SALT COD WITH BROCCOLI RAAB

BACALHAU COM GRELOS

Most weeknights, my mom or dad would throw together bacalhau com grelos for a quick dinner. They'd boil salt cod and greens and put them on a platter, family-style. I've elevated the dish here, using two-step techniques for each ingredient: searing then confiting the cod; blanching then sautéing the greens. Sure, it takes a little longer, but it now has all the warmth of my childhood meals with more complex textures.

SERVES 4

extra-virgin olive oil	as needed
Basic Salt Cod (page 26)	4 fillets (6 ounces/170 g each)
Broccoli Raab with Garlic and Red Chile Flakes (page 175)	1 recipe
sherry vinegar	to taste
yuzu or lemon	1, for serving
Maldon sea salt	for serving

Heat a cast-iron grill pan or skillet over high heat until hot. Coat with oil and add the salt cod, smooth-side down. Cook until golden brown, then carefully transfer to a sauté pan that can hold the salt cod in a single layer, browned-side up.

Add enough oil to cover the salt cod and bring the oil to 135°F (57°C) over medium heat. Cook the salt cod, adjusting the heat to maintain the oil temperature, until its internal temperature reaches 130°F (55°C) and a cake tester pierces the salt cod with no resistance, about 15 minutes. Carefully transfer to paper towels to drain and gently pat dry.

Divide the broccoli raab and salt cod among four serving plates. Drizzle with oil and vinegar to taste, then zest the yuzu or lemon directly on top. Sprinkle with a little Maldon salt and serve immediately.

SALT COD WITH SMASHED POTATOES AND SPRING ONIONS

BACALHAU COM BATATAS A MORRO

Potatoes and salt cod are a common combination for good reason: The creamy sweetness of the potatoes complements the savory fish. Here, cooking both in olive oil brings the elements together while lightly caramelized spring onions add another layer of natural sweetness.

SERVES 4

Basic Salt Cod (page 26)	4 fillets (6 ounces/170 g each)
Warm Smashed Potatoes (page 196)	1 recipe, cooking oil reserved
spring onions (see Note)	5, thin outer purple layers removed
unsalted butter	1 tablespoon
extra-virgin olive oil	2 tablespoons, plus more as needed
kosher salt	to taste
lemon wedge	1
fresh parsley leaves	2 tablespoons, torn
pitted Kalamata olives	5, quartered lengthwise
fresh lemon thyme leaves	½ teaspoon
pimentón (smoked sweet paprika)	½ teaspoon
fleur de sel	to taste
fig or balsamic vinegar	to taste

Put the salt cod, smooth-side up, in a sauté pan or saucepan just big enough to hold the fillets in one layer. Pour the potato-cooking oil through a fine-mesh sieve into the pan. Discard the garlic and herbs. If there isn't enough oil to cover the fish, add more. Cook the salt cod, adjusting the heat to maintain the oil temperature at 135°F (57°C), until its internal temperature reaches 130°F (55°C) and a cake tester pierces the salt cod with no resistance, about 15 minutes. Carefully transfer to paper towels to drain and gently pat dry.

Meanwhile, cut the onions lengthwise in quarters, then crosswise into ¼-inch (6-mm) slices. Heat the butter and 1 tablespoon of the oil over medium heat until the butter foams and bubbles. Add the onions and a generous pinch of kosher salt. Cook, stirring and scraping so you don't get any color on the onions, until they're almost translucent but still have a little crunch, about 3 minutes. They should still have their rounded shape. Squeeze some lemon juice over the onions, then fold in the parsley, olives, thyme, pimentón, and remaining 1 tablespoon oil.

Arrange the potatoes and salt cod on serving plates and spoon the onion mixture on top. Sprinkle fleur de sel all over and drizzle with a little vinegar and olive oil.

NOTE *If you can't find spring onions, you can use 1¼ cups (150 g) diced white onions instead and cook them longer, until they're completely tender. Spring onions are very mild, so I keep them crunchy. Mature white ones are more aggressive and taste better fully cooked.*

SALT COD, POTATO, AND EGG CASSEROLE

extra-virgin olive oil	as needed
white onions	2 small, quartered and very thinly sliced
garlic cloves	6, thinly sliced
fresh bay leaves	2, notches torn every ½ inch (12 mm)
kosher salt and freshly ground black pepper	to taste
Basic Salt Cod (page 26)	2 ounces (360 g), flaked into ½-inch (12-mm) pieces
Yukon gold potatoes	2 large
pitted Kalamata olives	½ cup, sliced crosswise, plus more for garnish
hard-boiled eggs	2 large, peeled and cut into ⅓-inch (8-mm) slices
fresh parsley leaves	¼ cup (7 g), very finely chopped

BACALHAU À GOMES DE SÁ

When I developed this recipe for the book, I couldn't stop digging into the Dutch oven and downing it by the forkful. I stuck to tradition here because you can't beat the delicious, comforting classic mix of sweet onions and potatoes with savory salt cod and olives pressed into a homey casserole.

SERVES 4

Preheat the oven to 325°F (165°C) with an oven rack set 6 inches (15 cm) from the broiler and one set in the center.

Heat a small (4-quart/3.8-L) cocotte or Dutch oven over medium heat. Coat the bottom with oil. Add the onions, garlic, bay leaves, and a big pinch of salt. Stir well, cover, and cook, stirring occasionally, until the onions are golden brown and very tender, about 10 minutes.

Meanwhile, cover the salt cod with oil in a medium skillet. Heat over medium heat, stirring gently, until heated through, about 1 minute.

Peel the potatoes and use a mandoline to cut them lengthwise into 1/16-inch (2-mm) slices. Don't rinse them; you want all that starch.

Transfer the onions to a bowl. Discard the bay leaves. Coat the bottom of the cocotte with oil and sprinkle salt and pepper over the oil. Cover the bottom of the cocotte with a layer of potatoes, overlapping the slices slightly. Season with salt, then cover with a thin layer of the onions and 1 tablespoon of the olives. Now layer potatoes, salt, pepper, oil, onions, salt, olives, and 1 cup (180 g) of the salt cod. Use a spatula to press down hard on the layers. Top with a layer of the egg slices, drizzle with oil, sprinkle with pepper, and add another layer of potatoes. Press hard again. For the final layering: add salt, oil, pepper, and the last of the onions, olives, salt cod, egg slices, and potatoes. Sprinkle with salt and pepper, drizzle with oil, and press down hard with your hand to get it as compact and even as possible.

Cover and bake on the center rack until the top is lightly browned and the potatoes are tender, 35 to 40 minutes. Spoon out any excess oil, then sprinkle with the parsley and more sliced olives. Adjust the oven to the broil setting. Broil the casserole until the top is golden brown. Let cool slightly before cutting into pieces.

SALT COD AND CHICKPEA SALAD

Beans and seafood are one of the most popular pairings in Portugal. Growing up, I often ate a version of this at home. I still do now: The combination of meaty chickpeas and bacalhau with crisp greens makes a great light lunch.

SERVES 4

extra-virgin olive oil	2 tablespoons, plus more to taste
Bacon-Braised Chickpeas (page 191)	4 cups (660 g)
Basic Salt Cod (page 26)	2 cups flaked (360 g)
Pickled Shallots (page 201)	2 tablespoons
fresh parsley leaves	2 teaspoons, finely chopped
freshly grated orange zest	¼ teaspoon
sherry vinegar	6 teaspoons, plus more to taste
kosher salt and freshly ground white pepper	to taste
baby watercress or arugula leaves	2 cups (85 g)
Parsley Oil (page 239)	to taste
Maldon sea salt	to taste

Heat the olive oil in a medium saucepan over medium-low heat. Add the chickpeas and salt cod and heat, stirring gently, to get the chill out of both. When they're warm, toss in the shallots, parsley, zest, and 4 teaspoons of the vinegar. Season with kosher salt and pepper.

In a medium bowl, lightly coat the greens with olive oil and toss with the remaining 2 teaspoons vinegar. Season with kosher salt and pepper and more olive oil and vinegar, if desired.

Divide the chickpea mixture among serving plates, plating them in a 6-inch (15-cm) ring mold, if desired. Drizzle with parsley oil and sprinkle with Maldon salt. Top with the greens and serve.

SALT COD WITH RAMPS, SWEET PEAS, AND LINGUIÇA

When Aldea opened in the early spring of 2009, I wanted to celebrate the first arrival of ramps and peas with Portuguese flavors. This combination of linguiça and salt cod does just that.

SERVES 4

yellow mustard seeds	1 teaspoon
cumin seeds	1 teaspoon
whole black peppercorns	1 teaspoon
fenugreek seeds	¾ teaspoon
dried curry leaf	½
ground turmeric	1 teaspoon
kosher salt and freshly ground white pepper	to taste
peas	1½ cups (216 g) shelled fresh or thawed frozen
extra-virgin olive oil	as needed
Basic Salt Cod (page 26)	4 fillets (6 ounces/170 g each)
linguiça	¼ cup (56 g) ⅛-inch- (3-mm-) thick slices
ramps	4 bunches (½ pound/225 g), leaves only
lemon thyme leaves	1½ teaspoons
chives	1½ teaspoons thinly sliced

In a small skillet, combine the mustard seeds, cumin, peppercorns, and fenugreek. Toast over medium heat, shaking the pan occasionally, until fragrant. Remove from the heat and let cool completely. Transfer to a spice grinder or mortar and pestle, along with the curry leaf and turmeric, and finely grind. Leftover spice mixture can be stored in an airtight container for up to 3 days.

If you're using fresh peas, fill a large bowl with ice and water. Bring a large saucepan of water to a boil and salt it generously. Add the peas and cook, stirring occasionally, until bright green and crisp-tender, 3 to 4 minutes. Immediately transfer to the ice water. When they are cool, drain well.

Choose a medium sauté pan that will fit the salt cod snugly in a single layer and fill it with oil to a depth of 2 inches (5 cm). Bring to 135°F (57°C) over medium heat. Add the salt cod, smooth-side up, and cook, adjusting the heat to maintain the oil temperature, until its internal temperature reaches 130°F (55°C) and a cake tester pierces the salt cod with no resistance, about 15 minutes. Carefully transfer to paper towels to drain and gently pat dry.

Meanwhile, heat a medium sauté pan over medium heat. Lightly coat with oil and add the linguiça. Cook, stirring occasionally, until the slices curl slightly and turn golden brown. Add the ramp leaves and cook, stirring, until wilted. Stir in the cooked fresh or thawed frozen peas, thyme, and chives. Season with salt and pepper. Divide the mixture among four serving plates. Top with the salt cod and dust the tops of the fish with the spice mixture. Serve immediately.

SALT COD CONFIT, CORIANDER DASHI, SHIITAKE, AND LITCHI

My love of Japanese food converges with my Portuguese heritage here: clean savory dashi with briny salt cod. The caramelized litchis add a sweet, interesting crunch.

SERVES 4

extra-virgin olive oil	1 quart (960 ml), plus more as needed
garlic cloves	5, crushed
fresh thyme	5 sprigs
fresh parsley	5 sprigs
fresh bay leaves	2, notches torn every ½ inch (12 mm)
Basic Salt Cod (page 26)	4 fillets (6 ounces/170 g each)
baby shiitake mushrooms	16, stems trimmed
kosher salt and freshly ground white pepper	to taste
fresh lemon juice	to taste
fresh litchis	8, peeled, seeded, and quartered
fresh cilantro leaves	for garnish
Coriander Dashi (page 231)	4 cups (946 ml), warmed

In a large saucepan, combine the oil, garlic, thyme, parsley, and bay leaves. Bring them to 150°F (65°C) over medium-low heat. Adjust the heat to maintain the temperature for 1 hour.

Strain the oil through a fine-mesh sieve into a deep skillet that will hold the salt cod in a single layer; discard the solids. Bring the oil to 135°F (57°C) over medium heat. Add the salt cod, smooth-side up, and cook, adjusting the heat to maintain the oil temperature, until its internal temperature reaches 130°F (55°C) and a cake tester pierces the salt cod with no resistance, about 15 minutes. Carefully transfer to paper towels to drain and gently pat dry.

Heat a large skillet over medium-high heat. Coat with 1 tablespoon oil. Add the mushrooms, season lightly with salt and pepper, and sauté, tossing, until lightly browned. Sprinkle with lemon juice. Keep warm.

Heat another skillet over medium-high heat. Coat with 1 tablespoon oil. Add the litchis and caramelize, stirring, until deep brown. Keep warm.

In each of four serving bowls, arrange a salt cod fillet in the center. Scatter the mushrooms and cilantro all around and top each with litchis. Pour the hot dashi around the fish and serve immediately.

REDISCOVERING MY CULINARY ROOTS

2013 | FERREIRÓS DO DÃO

I can't give you the address of the best restaurant in my family's village, because it doesn't have one—and it isn't an actual restaurant. But it *is* where you can taste pure Portuguese cooking—the kind of food we grew up eating in our social clubs, after church, at weddings and baptisms, and under huge tents on festival days. Just drive north toward Viseu, of the Dão-Lafões centro region, and follow the signs for the small city Tondela, then for my village, Ferreirós do Dão. Creep down the hairpin turns through the steep eucalyptus groves and over the Moorish stone bridge that spans the River Dão. Now, finding the actual restaurant is like following the stations of the cross: Start at the central church's cross, the highest point in the village. Head east and look for a Romanesque column topped with a cross in the middle of the road, then drive to a heavy, squat medieval cross off to the side. Across the way is a low-slung white stucco building with a single Super Bock flag hanging over the door. You're there: Casa do Povo. (If you start driving down a hill, you've gone too far. You're now at my aunt's house.)

Show up Sunday to Thursday and you're out of luck. The chef, Joao "Faia" Martina, cooks only on Friday and Saturday nights and only after 7 p.m. Faia grew up in Ferreirós do Dão and, like half the village of my parents' generation, moved to Connecticut in the seventies. When he got to Danbury, he cooked at his restaurant and the social club where the Portuguese-American community gathered to drink and eat after their long days working at the local factories. And I swear he catered every wedding of every Portuguese-American couple in the state of Connecticut.

Faia was the first chef I ever met. (His wife was his "sous chef.") I was nine or ten and I wanted to see the club's kitchen. Even before I walked through the swinging doors, I could hear him yelling. Once I got in there, I was hit with the crazy heat, the smell of frying potatoes so heavy I could feel it on my skin, and Faia's string of curses. Rumor had it he once screamed loud enough to blow the hat off a cook's head. Twenty-five years of that intensity in the kitchen led to an aneurysm and the doctor ordering him to retire.

He moved back to Ferreirós do Dão to slow down the pace, to be done with his chef's life. And this is where it gets good: He couldn't do it. Here's a guy who just can't stop cooking. Faia was supposed to relax, but he saw the social club in Ferreirós sitting empty and he started going to the market and he got behind the stove again. And everyone came. No menu, not even a blackboard listing specials. He just gets what looks best at the market and nails it. My cousin told me that you can tell Faia what you're craving—his octopus or shrimp or whatever—and he'll go out, buy it, and cook it when you come in.

Faia's food is as good today as it was thirty years ago, maybe better. He's stopped screaming—now there's this calm Yoda half-smile under his gray mustache. His wife's still there by his side in the kitchen, her hair as perfectly styled as his is wild. In the summer, his daughters come back from Connecticut. They're still his servers, and they're still bickering about who gets to leave first. Pretty soon, their teenage kids will start helping out, but for now, the girls are playing foosball at the front of the club and the boys are out in the field with the soccer ball.

Sitting under the streamers and balloons from the last party Faia catered, I feel like I'm back home. His daughter brings me a Coke, like old times, plus a bottle of vinho verde. Then, a huge family-style platter of seafood and potatoes arrives. The stainless-steel tray is loaded with bacalhau frito smothered in soft onions and red peppers. It's set in the middle, like the love child of the fried potatoes and fresh seafood. On one side are a thick-cut perca fish steak from a local fisherman, a whole dorade, fat octopus tentacles, and curls of cuttlefish, all smoky from the grill. Under the fish are whole gold potatoes, smashed to pucks and soaking up the fish's juices. Anchoring the other end are Faia's signature potatoes: flat paving-stone slabs browned around the edges, perfectly crisp, and not at all greasy.

Genevieve and I are still full from our double lunch, but this is the kind of food you find an appetite for. Even though all of the seafood is essentially prepared in the same way, each item stands out. The perca's fatty and silky; the dorade, flaky yet meaty. The cuttlefish has just the right chew, and the octopus is perfectly tender. The charred bits add a rich depth to complement the fresh and light raw onions, garlic, cilantro, and parsley on top. The bacalhau's a progression of goodness: From the crunchy corners to the juicy center, the sea-salty fish is balanced by the tangy-sweet pepper garnish. Everything on the platter is just simple food. And that's what makes it so great. Faia's a chef who's skilled enough—and smart enough—to know that if you get the best products, you've got to let them shine.

We polish off the whole platter because it's delicious, but also maybe because I'm still terrified of Faia yelling at me for not finishing my food. Yeah, he used to do that. But not tonight. As we talk, I can see how content he is. And I feel the same way I did when I was a kid: I want to be this guy. I want to run my kitchen and feed my community my whole career, retire in some beautiful place, and just keep cooking, whenever I want, whatever I want. Faia's a true chef. Not classically trained, no Michelin stars, but at his core, he can't—he won't—stop cooking. He just wants to make good food and feed people. So do I.

Chef Faia's seafood feast, from left: fried potatoes, bacalhau frito, perca fish steak, cuttlefish, dorade, and octopus.

CHAPTER 2

THE SEA: SHELLFISH AND FISH

LIKE FATHER, LIKE SON

1990 | DANBURY

By the time I was a teenager, I resented my dad for making me spend my weekends with him. Over the years, he had bought, fixed up, and rented out properties in our central Connecticut neighborhood. And I was expected to help him. My friends' parents let them do whatever they wanted on weekends. Sleep in, play basketball, hang out doing nothing together. That was all I wanted. But on Saturday mornings, my dad would holler into my room, "Get up! Let's go!" He'd usually leave first, before I could drag myself out of bed. By the time I made it to the site, I could feel my dad's disappointment across the lawn I should've mowed hours earlier.

Once there, I'd willfully do a half-ass job, just to piss off my dad. When he checked the rooms I painted, he looked at each wall molding to make sure the lines were clean. Mine weren't. He's a real craftsman who trained as a mason in France and Portugal, and a ferociously hard worker who juggled a full-time factory job with these side projects to give us a better life in America. But I didn't appreciate that then, didn't really care that I'd eventually learn from his work ethic and perfectionism and use them to build my career.

Now I can see how deep his influence runs, even in the kitchen. Even though women commonly do the cooking in Portugal, both in restaurants and homes, my dad was as comfortable behind the stove as my mom. And he had a few specialties she couldn't touch. Among them was his shrimp alhinho, a traditional garlicky seared shrimp dish. He'd build the flavors, layer by layer, and he never overcooked the shrimp, taking them off the heat at the height of their plump juiciness.

When we opened Aldea, we weren't sure how we could take that weeknight meal and turn it into a refined restaurant dish. We didn't want to introduce new seasonings because the essence of the dish is simply the shrimp with garlic, herbs, and smoked paprika. So we did what my dad had been teaching me all these years: We just made it better. To intensify the shrimp, we make a concentrated jus from the heads. Then we sear the bodies to caramelize them before poaching them in garlic-infused paprika oil. The jus and oil run into each other on the plate, and we always spoon on extra for sopping up with good bread, just the way we did at home.

Top: Portugal's president Aníbal Cavaco Silva posed with me and my dad after a luncheon at Aldea in 2012. Bottom: We were regulars at my aunt's restaurant in Danbury, Connecticut.

47

GARLIC SEARED SHRIMP

SHRIMP ALHINHO

Aside from being a masterful carpenter and stone-wall builder, my dad makes a mean shrimp alhinho. At Aldea, we take his go-to dish one step further by making an intense sauce with the shrimp heads. Even now, well into retirement, he cooks his version with his cane in one hand while he stirs with the other. If that isn't badass, I don't know what is.

SERVES 4

extra-virgin olive oil	as needed
large (20/30 count) shrimp (see Note)	20, peeled and deveined
garlic cloves	6, minced
pimentón (sweet smoked paprika)	1½ teaspoons
fresh parsley leaves	1 tablespoon, chopped
fresh cilantro leaves	1 tablespoon, chopped, plus more for garnish
fresh lemon juice	½ teaspoon
Shrimp Essence (page 232)	1 cup (240 ml), or to taste
paprika filaments (see Notes)	for garnish

Heat a large skillet over high heat until very hot. Lightly coat the bottom with oil and heat until lightly smoking. Add half of the shrimp in a single layer. Cook just until golden and orange, about 10 seconds, then flip them quickly. Cook for 10 seconds more and immediately transfer to a plate. Repeat with the remaining shrimp.

Reduce the heat to medium-high and add ¼ cup (60 ml) more oil. Add the garlic and cook, stirring, until light golden but not browned, about 2 minutes. Stir in the pimentón, then return the shrimp to the pan. Adjust the heat to bring the oil to a slow bubble and poach the shrimp for 1 minute. Fold in the parsley, cilantro, and lemon juice.

Divide the shrimp among four serving plates. Spoon the pan sauce with the garlic and herbs over the shrimp. Spoon the shrimp essence over and around the shrimp. Garnish with the paprika filaments and more cilantro.

NOTES *I looked far and wide to source the best shrimp for this dish. At the restaurant, the shrimp I use has an intense natural brininess, so I don't need to salt it at all. If you're using a sweet shrimp or a mild variety, give it a good sprinkle of salt before searing.*

Paprika filaments look like extra-long saffron threads and add a hint of spice to the dish. You can find them online or at specialty stores.

THE WAY TO EAT SEAFOOD

2013 | LISBON

I stumble off the red-eye in Lisbon for a week of tasting Portugal's cuisine for this book and I know exactly where to start. After a few shots of espresso and a cold shower at the Bairro Alto Hotel, I climb into the backseat of my friend Mário Neves's car. He and his wife, Margarita, drove down from Évora to join me for lunch at Cervejaria Ramiro, my favorite restaurant in the city. We wind away from Bairro Alto's beautiful city square and polished restaurants into the grittier downtown. Wedged between Chinese markets and Indian spice shops, this seafood institution spans a few storefronts and the line to get in usually extends longer than that.

But we roll in during the late afternoon, after the lunch crowd and before the dinner crush. As soon as we walk through the door, the owner, Pedro Gonçalves, welcomes us. Mário's been a Portuguese wine distributor (and Ramiro regular) for years and you can't miss him, with his bushy, soaring white eyebrows. Pedro's happy to see me, too, because I'm there every time I'm in Lisbon, and I've sent countless chefs to dine there.

Ramiro is the place for killer seafood. They understand that the way to serve seafood is to source the best you can possibly find, get it as fresh as possible, and treat it simply. They even share that value in their pricing: Their dishes cost the weight of the seafood you eat.

I was lucky enough to be there during percebes season. Percebes are gooseneck barnacles that Ramiro buys from divers who go dangerously deep to pluck the juiciest ones around Belingus Island. Back in the kitchen, they are steamed with sea water to retain their briny flavor. They taste like the essence of the ocean—sweeter than lobster, with a more substantial chew than razor clams. Ramiro's steamed whelks, which they bring to the table with hooks for pulling the meat out of the conical spiky shells, are as tasty and even chewier.

We move on to gamba, small shrimp caught off the Algarve coast a hundred miles south just that morning. Again, they're simply steamed with their heads and shells to capture their tender sweetness, then sprinkled with coarse sea salt. A little more savory and a lot more meaty are the half-foot langostins caught further north on the coast. Then comes the icing on the cake: carabineiros from Mozambique. These huge brick-red prawns taste like a more complex, meaty lobster and spew a flood of delicious juices when we pull the heads from the bodies.

When Ramiro does season its seafood, they add just enough to highlight, not mask, its natural flavors. Their amêijoas à Bulhão Pato is all about the fat little clams; the vinho verde sauce studded with garlic and herbs serves only to make them that much more succulent. The key to that dish—and all seafood dishes, for that matter—is to soak up the juices left on the plate with pao com manteiga, crusty hot buttered toast. It makes the best seafood even better.

Clockwise from top: the restaurant's entrance; whelks; Pedro showing me langostins; carabineiros; classic table setting.

MOZAMBIQUE SHRIMP AND OKRA WITH PIRI PIRI

Piri piri is the national hot sauce of Portugal and commonly used in the country's former colonies, too. In Mozambique, okra and tomatoes are stewed with shrimp in this fiery dish. I've abandoned the old-school slimy okra and rubbery shrimp textures by grilling the okra and shrimp until they're both smoky and crisp.

SERVES 4

okra pods	16, halved lengthwise
garlic cloves	2, very thinly sliced; 3, minced
pimentón (sweet smoked paprika)	pinch
extra-virgin olive oil	as needed
beefsteak tomatoes	2 ripe
white onion	½ medium, finely diced
fresh bay leaf	1, notches torn every ½ inch (12 mm)
kosher salt and freshly ground white pepper	to taste
tomato paste	1 tablespoon
Piri Piri (page 236)	3 tablespoons, plus more for serving
Shrimp Essence (page 232)	½ cup (120 ml)
extra-large (15/20 count) shrimp	16, peeled and deveined
freshly grated orange zest	½ teaspoon
freshly grated lime zest	½ teaspoon
fresh cilantro	4 teaspoons finely chopped

Prepare a grill by heating a mixture of all-natural briquettes and hardwood lump charcoal until very hot.

In a large bowl, toss the okra with the sliced garlic, pimentón, and enough oil to coat. Let stand until you're ready to grill.

Meanwhile, fill a large bowl with ice and water. Bring a large saucepan of water to a boil. Slit an "x" in the base of each tomato and drop in the boiling water. Let sit for 10 seconds, then transfer to the ice water until cool. Peel, seed, and cut into ¼-inch (6-mm) dice.

In a medium cast-iron cocotte or Dutch oven, heat ¼ cup (60 ml) oil over medium heat. Add the onion, minced garlic, and bay leaf and season with salt. Cook, stirring occasionally, until the onion is translucent and tender, about 5 minutes.

Stir in the tomatoes and tomato paste and season with salt. Simmer until the mixture is thickened, about 8 minutes. Stir in the piri piri and shrimp essence and bring to a simmer. Continue simmering while you cook the shrimp and okra.

Coat the shrimp with oil and season with salt and pepper. Place the shrimp and okra on the grill grate in a single layer. Cook, turning occasionally, until the shrimp are just opaque throughout and the okra are blackened in spots.

Fold the shrimp and okra into the simmering sauce; discard the bay leaf. Season with salt and pepper and top with the zests and cilantro. Drizzle with oil and serve with more piri piri on the side.

SAFFRON RICE WITH SEARED SHRIMP AND FOIE GRAS

When I cooked as the chef de cuisine at Tocqueville, I began experimenting with classic Portuguese dishes, modernizing them with what I'd learned professionally. Here, I applied the risotto technique of toasting the rice first and this dish became a hit. There are so many great textures going on—the bite of the al dente rice, creamy foie gras, chewy shrimp—all bound with the heady fragrance of saffron.

SERVES 4 TO 6

extra-virgin olive oil	as needed
Refogado (page 235)	½ cup (120 ml)
saffron	¼ teaspoon
cebolla rice	2 cups (13 ounces/364 g)
dry white vinho verde	1 cup (240 ml)
Chicken Stock (page 226)	2 quarts (2 L), hot
kosher salt and freshly ground white pepper	to taste
Shrimp Essence (page 232)	2 cups (480 ml), hot
jumbo (10/15 count) shrimp	1 pound (455 g), heads intact, bodies peeled and deveined
foie gras	8 ounces (1 inch/2.5 cm thick), patted dry, lightly scored
fresh thyme leaves	1 teaspoon
unsalted butter	4 tablespoons (55 g)
freshly grated lime zest	1 teaspoon
Maldon sea salt	for serving
lemon wedges	for serving

Heat a large saucepan over medium heat and generously coat the bottom of the pan with oil. Add the refogado and cook, stirring, for 1 minute. Add the saffron and rice and cook, stirring, until the rice is toasted and fragrant, about 6 minutes. The rice should be well-coated with oil, so add more if needed.

Add the vinho verde and cook, stirring, until evaporated. Add 4 cups (1 L) of the stock and cook, stirring, for 1 minute. Continue simmering without stirring for 15 minutes, then stir in 2 cups (480 ml) more stock, scraping down the sides of the pan. Season with a pinch of kosher salt and continue stirring until the stock is absorbed. Repeat with the remaining stock. Stir in the shrimp essence and keep the mixture warm over low heat.

Meanwhile, heat two large skillets over high heat. Season the shrimp and the foie gras with kosher salt and pepper. Coat both skillets with oil, then add the shrimp to one pan and the foie gras to the other. Cook until both are well browned on the bottom, gently pressing to help them sear, about 1 minute for the foie gras and 2 minutes for the shrimp. Flip both over and brown the other sides really well, about 1 minute for the foie gras and 2 minutes for the shrimp. Remove the skillets from the heat and divide the thyme and butter between the skillets. Turn the foie gras and shrimp to coat with the butter.

Transfer the rice to a serving platter or four serving dishes and drizzle with oil. Cut the foie gras into 1-inch (2.5-cm) slices and place on top of the rice, along with the shrimp and their thyme butter. Sprinkle with the lime zest and Maldon salt and squeeze lemon juice all over. Serve immediately.

SEAFOOD RICE

kosher salt and freshly ground white pepper	to taste
Refogado (page 235)	1 tablespoon
extra-virgin olive oil	as needed
Carolina Gold long-grain rice	1 cup (185 g)
Shrimp or Lobster Stock (page 232)	3 cups (720 ml)
lobster	1 tail and 2 claws
dry white vinho verde	1 cup (240 ml)
garlic cloves	2, smashed
fresh cilantro	2 sprigs, plus more finely chopped for garnish
Prince Edward Island mussels	8
littleneck clams	8
sea scallops	4 large, tough muscles removed
large (20/30 count) shrimp	8, peeled and deveined
West Coast sea urchins	8 tongues (see page 78)
freshly grated lime zest	for serving
fleur de sel	for serving

ARROZ DE MARISCOS

I had the best version of this classic at Cervejaria da Esquina in Lisbon. There, the chef served the fragrant rice and seafood in enough broth to make the mixture resemble a stew. I've kept the sauciness, but thickened it to make the dish taste even richer. In addition to cooking the rice to just the right point—a little past al dente—I cook each type of seafood separately to optimize their textures. When everything is combined at the end, all the flavors meld together into a bowl of elevated comfort.

SERVES 4

Bring a large saucepan of generously salted water to a boil. Meanwhile, in a heavy 3-quart (2.8-L) stockpot, heat the refogado and 2 tablespoons oil over medium-low heat, then stir in the rice. Season with salt. Cook, stirring, until the rice is toasted, 3 to 4 minutes. Stir in ½ cup (120 ml) of the stock. Cover, reduce the heat to low, and simmer for 5 minutes. Stir in the remaining 2½ cups (600 ml) stock. Bring to a simmer, cover, and cook just until a soft bite remains, about 15 minutes.

While the rice simmers, drop the lobster tail and claws into the boiling water. Cook the tail for 4 minutes and the claws for 6 minutes. Transfer to a cutting board. When cool enough to handle, shell and cut the meat into chunks.

Divide the vinho verde, garlic, and cilantro sprigs between two medium saucepans. Bring to a boil. Add the mussels to one pan and the clams to the other. Cover and cook just until the shellfish open. Immediately transfer to a plate. Strain the cooking liquids through a fine-mesh sieve and reserve.

With a sharp knife, score both sides of each scallop in a crosshatch pattern. Season with salt and pepper. Heat a large skillet over high heat until it is very hot. Lightly coat with oil and heat until lightly smoking. Add the scallops in a single layer. Cook, pressing flat with a spatula, until brown, about 1 minute per side. Transfer to a plate. Repeat with the shrimp, cooking just until orange, about 10 seconds per side.

Gently stir ¼ cup (60 ml) of the reserved shellfish liquid into the rice. Season with salt and pepper. Fold in the lobster, mussels, clams, shrimp, and scallops and heat for 2 minutes. Arrange the sea urchin tongues on top. Drizzle with oil and sprinkle with the lime zest, chopped cilantro, and fleur de sel.

NORTH BY NORTHWEST

2013 | PORTO

On the drive up to Porto, I hit a wall of fog so thick I can't see more than a car's length ahead of me. After a second, I realize it's not fog, but smoke from a nearby forest fire. I smell the burning eucalyptus and know I'm heading into the region of heartier, more rustic cuisine. Soon after the air clears, I coast past the series of bridges, alternating between modern minimalist and ornate latticework, that lead to Portugal's second-largest city. That meeting of old and new continues when I pull into an underground parking lot that's hidden beneath a beautiful old square and equipped with a progressive automated pay system.

One of the first things I see in the city is a big Galo de Barcelos hanging in front of a jewelry store. The iconic rooster statue, with a crimson comb like a pompadour, originated with a seventeenth-century legend from the northwestern Braga district. In the story, a convicted man claims his innocence will be proven when a dead rooster crows at his hanging. Sure enough, the dead rooster crows and the man is set free. And a symbol is born. Throughout Portugal, rooster statuettes are sold, their bodies painted black and decorated with bright spots and flowers. At Aldea, I had displayed a few small ones. Now, I want to buy the one at the jewelry store for my chef's counter. I convince the store owners to sell it to me since it is part of their décor and not an item for sale, then I continue on to the waterfront.

Even though it's the middle of July, it's as crisp as a fall day. The sky's overcast and the breeze from the Douro River adds to the chill in the air. Across the river, the port houses—Dow's, Taylor's, Sandemann's—are lined up like a streaming ad for our greatest export. I walk past the souvenir vendors and the tour guides offering port-tasting cruises and wander through the small side streets until I get to the off-the-beaten-path Restaurante A Grade.

The homey mom-and-pop taberna is tucked away on a tiny, steep side street near a nursery school. If you eat on their storefront patio, you can wave to the toddlers skipping past. I opt for the warm, cozy dining room. Once inside, you feel like you've stepped back in time. With the exception of the TV blaring parliamentary proceedings, the room is all rustic wood and classic blue-and-white Portuguese tile. Porto is known for rich dishes like francesinha, a sandwich layered with ham, sausages, steak, tomato, and cheese, then smothered in beer sauce. Because the city's both on the water and further north, its cuisine is defined by more substantial seafood preparations. That's why I came to A Grade, to try their signature polvo assado no forno, oven-roasted octopus.

CONTINUED >>

Traditional, casual eateries and modern new restaurants line the small side streets of Porto.

I'm welcomed like family by the eager young server, who pours a clean, spritzy vinho verde, and the gray-haired gentleman, who runs the room, cracking jokes with the men and charming the women. I start with one of the best bolos de bacalhau I've ever had. Where other versions of the salt cod fritter tend toward soft and creamy, this one has a substantial chew from the fish-packed filling. The fried baby sardines that follow are even better. They're like the Portuguese version of chips—shatteringly crisp, but far tastier. I pop them in, heads and all, amazed by how greaseless they are.

They're the ideal start to my main dish: polvo assado. When my butter knife slides through the octopus, I know it's going to be good. It turns out to be mind-blowing. As tender as it is, it still has a great chew. And the olive oil it's braised in is so intense that the octopus actually picks up the savory brine of olives. So do the potatoes cooked in the same terra-cotta casserole. I ask the server how they do it. He tells me matter-of-factly that the women in the kitchen simmer the tentacles with wine and aromatics, then roast them with baby potatoes and onions. Simple as that.

It isn't the time to dissect the dish or deconstruct it. I just follow suit with the regulars who fill the tables around me, all digging into their casseroles of polvo, spooning the side of fluffy saffron rice onto their plates. When I wipe every last drop of that unbelievable oil off my plate, I'm served a glass of aguardente, the Portuguese version of moonshine, on the house. I sip and let the food coma wash over me. Because that is what you call lunch.

Top: Classic Portuguese architecture surrounds Porto's main square. Bottom: My lunch at A Grade showcased the best of northern cuisine.

OCTOPUS CONFIT

Tender octopus is the foundation of many Portuguese dishes. I like to cook the tentacles really low and slow in aromatic olive oil to infuse them with an extra depth of richness.

SERVES 4

octopus tentacles	2½ pounds (1.2 kg)
carrot	1 medium, peeled and sliced
fennel bulb	1 medium, trimmed and thinly sliced
whole white peppercorns	1½ teaspoons
whole black peppercorns	1 tablespoon
coriander seeds	1 tablespoon
extra-virgin olive oil	as needed

Preheat the oven to 250°F (120°C).

Straddle a small roasting pan between two burners and place the octopus, carrot, fennel, white and black peppercorns, and coriander in the pan. Add enough oil to completely cover the octopus. Bring to a simmer over medium-high heat, then cover the pan tightly with foil.

Bake until the octopus is completely tender, 6 to 8 hours. The timing varies largely based on the octopus itself. Start checking at 6 hours; there should be very little resistance when it is pierced with a cake tester or thin-bladed knife. Transfer the octopus to a cutting board. Strain the oil through a fine-mesh sieve and reserve for another use; discard the solids. Use the octopus in Octopus and Black-Eyed Pea Salad (page 63) or another dish, or slice and serve on its own.

OCTOPUS AND BLACK-EYED PEA SALAD

To balance the meaty octopus and beans, I lighten this salad with greens, citrus, herbs, and vinegar. The end result tastes substantial enough to serve as a full meal, but would also be a great way to start a feast.

SERVES 4

Aromatic Black-Eyed Peas (page 190)	4 cups (660 g)
shallots	2, very thinly sliced
sherry vinegar	4 teaspoons, plus more to taste
extra-virgin olive oil	as needed
Octopus Confit (page 61)	4 (8-inch/20-cm) tentacles, cut into 1-inch (2.5-cm) chunks
fresh parsley leaves	¼ cup, finely chopped
fresh cilantro leaves	¼ cup, finely chopped
freshly grated lemon zest	1 teaspoon
fleur de sel	to taste
baby greens	for serving

If the peas are cold, toss them in a large saucepan with enough oil to lightly coat over medium heat until they reach room temperature. Transfer to a large bowl and toss with the shallots and vinegar.

Heat a large skillet over high heat until very hot. Lightly coat the bottom with oil and heat until lightly smoking. Add half of the octopus in a single layer. Cook just until browned and lightly caramelized, about 30 seconds, then flip quickly. Cook for 30 seconds more and immediately transfer to a large bowl. Repeat with the remaining octopus. Alternatively, lightly coat the octopus with oil and grill over medium-hot charcoal until charred.

Toss the octopus with the parsley, cilantro, and lemon zest. Season with fleur de sel. Toss in the greens and peas. Divide among four serving dishes. Season with oil, additional vinegar, and fleur de sel.

CLAMS STEAMED WITH VINHO VERDE, GARLIC, AND CILANTRO

AMÊIJOAS À BULHÃO PATO

A classic throughout Portugal, this is named for Bulhão Pato, a food-loving nineteenth-century Portuguese poet. No one really remembers his writing, but his namesake dish is legendary. It's the pure essence of the ocean here. This dish is so simple and delicious, I could eat it every day. Once I finish the clams, I like to spoon the sauce with the garlic and cilantro onto hunks of good crusty buttered and toasted bread.

SERVES 2

kosher salt	to taste
littleneck clams	12
extra-virgin olive oil	as needed
garlic cloves	2 large, very thinly sliced crosswise
fresh bay leaf	1, notches torn every ½ inch (12 mm)
dry white vinho verde	½ cup (120 ml)
fresh cilantro	2 sprigs plus ½ cup sliced leaves

Fill a bowl with cold water and dissolve enough salt in it to make it taste like the ocean. Submerge the clams in the water. Let them sit for 10 minutes or until they spit out their grit. You should see sand at the bottom of the bowl. Lift out the clams and transfer to a colander. With a stiff-bristled brush, scrub them vigorously until their shells are really clean.

Heat a medium saucepan over medium-low heat. Coat the bottom with oil and add the garlic and bay leaf. Cook, stirring continuously, until very aromatic, bubbling, and golden, about 4 minutes.

Add the clams and toss to coat in the mixture and get a sizzle going on them. Add the vinho verde and cilantro sprigs. Cover, raise the heat to medium-high, and cook, shaking the pan frequently, until the clams start to open. The liquid should be boiling vigorously. Start pulling out the early birds that open first and transfer them to a dish. Cover the pan again and continue cooking and pulling until all the clams open. After 5 minutes more, any clams that don't open are dead; throw them out.

Discard the bay leaf and cilantro sprigs. Strain the sauce into a large serving bowl. Swirl in a little olive oil, then fold in the clams and sliced cilantro. Serve immediately with plenty of crusty bread.

GOAN CUTTLEFISH COCONUT CURRY

Smelling this sauce brings back great memories of when Aldea first opened and we put this dish on the menu. It was my first foray into showcasing dishes inspired by Portugal's history of world exploration. Goa was a Portuguese province from the sixteenth to the twentieth century and much of its culture still exhibits that influence. On the flip side, this dish is influenced by Goa's setting on India's southwestern coast, where seafood comes generously spiced.

Cuttlefish, popular in Portuguese cuisine but underrated here, are in the octopus family and have a complex texture that's more toothsome than squid or calamari. Try to find the smallest ones possible for this recipe and clean them well, removing any cartilage, before cooking. Be sure to pick up squid ink from the fishmonger while you're there.

SERVES 6

SPECIAL EQUIPMENT:
> IMMERSION BLENDER

COCONUT SAUCE

baby cuttlefish	36 whole, rinsed
extra-virgin olive oil	3 tablespoons, plus more as needed
white onion	½ small, thinly sliced
garlic cloves	5, thinly sliced
fresh ginger	1 tablespoon thinly sliced
fresh lemongrass	1 stalk, thinly sliced
fresh bay leaf	1, notches torn every ½ inch (12 mm)
kosher salt	to taste
fresh Kaffir lime leaves	10, thinly sliced
coconut milk	2 (15-ounce/450-ml) cans
tamarind paste	1½ teaspoons
soy lechitin powder (optional; see Notes)	1 tablespoon

MAKE THE SAUCE: Pull the cuttlefish heads (with the tentacles) from the bodies. Trim the eyes off the heads and discard the eyes and the intestines. Pull out the central bones from the bodies and discard. Gently pull the flat wing pieces off the bodies and remove and discard the skin.

Refrigerate the cuttlefish heads and flat pieces until you are ready to sear; pat the cuttlefish bodies dry with paper towels. Heat a large stockpot over high heat until very hot. Coat the bottom with the 3 tablespoons oil and heat until lightly smoking. Add the bodies in a single layer. Cook until browned and caramelized, about 3 minutes per side.

Reduce the heat to medium. Add the onion, garlic, ginger, lemongrass, bay leaf, a generous pinch of salt, and enough oil so that the aromatics sizzle. Cook, stirring frequently, until the onion is caramelized but not colored, about 6 minutes. Add the lime leaves; cook, stirring, for 1 minute. Stir in the coconut milk, tamarind, and ½ cup (120 ml) water. Bring to a boil and simmer for 3 minutes, then stir in the soy lechitin powder, if using. Season with salt and simmer for 20 minutes.

CONTINUED >>

CUTTLEFISH CURRY

fresh cilantro	5 sprigs, plus leaves for garnish
bonito flakes	2 cups (28 g), plus more for garnish
fresh lime juice	1 tablespoon
Squid Ink Sauce (page 237)	2 tablespoons
kosher salt and freshly ground white pepper	to taste
extra-virgin olive oil	as needed
fresh lemon wedges	for serving
fleur de sel	for serving
Tomato Confit (page 243)	24 pieces
Herb Puree (page 238)	to taste
crushed red chile flakes	for serving

MAKE THE CURRY: Remove the coconut sauce from the heat and add the cilantro sprigs and bonito flakes. Let sit for 1 minute, then stir in the lime juice. Strain through a fine-mesh sieve, pressing on the solids to extract as much liquid as possible. Discard the solids. Foam the sauce with an immersion blender until frothy. Transfer half of the sauce to a small saucepan and set over low heat. Whisk in the squid ink sauce and keep warm. Reserve the remaining sauce.

With a sharp paring knife, score the cuttlefish heads and flat pieces in a crosshatch pattern. Season with salt and pepper. Heat a large skillet over high heat until very hot. Lightly coat the bottom with oil and heat until lightly smoking. Add the cuttlefish heads and flat pieces, smooth-sides down, in a single layer. Cook, pressing with a spatula, until golden brown, about 1 minute per side. Transfer to a cutting board and cut each piece in half. Squeeze with lemon juice and season with fleur de sel.

Divide the squid ink sauce among six serving dishes. Divide the cuttle-fish and tomato confit among the dishes. Froth the curry sauce again and divide among the dishes. Drizzle with the herb puree, sprinkle cilantro leaves, additional bonito flakes, and chile flakes on top, and serve immediately.

NOTES *All of the Asian ingredients here—lemongrass, Kaffir lime leaves, tamarind paste, bonito flakes—can be found online or in Asian markets.*

Soy lecithin, available in specialty markets and online, helps the sauce froth to a smooth, airy consistency. It's not necessary, but gives the dish a professional finish.

SEARED SCALLOPS WITH APPLE-WATERCRESS SAUCE

Fresh and green, this sauce is the perfect accent to simply seared sweet scallops. It's also great with Octopus Confit (page 61) or seared shrimp.

SERVES 4

extra-virgin olive oil	as needed
white onion	½ medium, very thinly sliced
kosher salt and freshly ground white pepper	to taste
dry white vinho verde	½ cup (120 ml)
watercress	1 bunch (4 ounces/112 g)
spinach leaves	1 cup (1 ounce/30 g) packed
apple balsamic vinegar	1 tablespoon
Ultra-Tex (optional; see Note)	1 teaspoon
sea scallops	20 large, tough muscles removed

Heat a small saucepan over medium heat. Coat with oil, then add the onion and a pinch of salt. Sweat, stirring occasionally, until the onion is soft. Deglaze with the vinho verde, stirring until the liquid evaporates.

Transfer the onion mixture to a blender, along with the watercress, spinach, vinegar, Ultra-Tex (if using), ¼ cup (60 ml) water, and a pinch of salt. Puree until smooth. With the machine running, drizzle in enough oil to create an emulsion, tasting occasionally to determine the amount you want. Season with salt.

With a sharp paring knife, score both sides of each scallop in a cross-hatch pattern. Season with salt and pepper. Heat a large skillet over high heat until very hot. Lightly coat the bottom with oil and heat until lightly smoking. Add the scallops in a single layer, working in batches if necessary. Cook, pressing flat with a spatula, until brown, about 1 minute per side.

Divide the watercress sauce among four serving plates and top each with 5 scallops. Serve immediately.

NOTE *Ultra-Tex is available through professional cooking supply stores. It helps the sauce here emulsify and gives it body.*

RED SNAPPER WITH SHELLFISH, TOMATO, AND SAFFRON

CALDEIRADA

In Portugal, caldeirada is our answer to bouillabaisse. Instead of doing it traditionally as a one-pot mix, I've intensified the flavors as both a sauce and garnish and added the delicate fish and crab at the very end. Sometimes, I serve it with shrimp, mussels, or other shellfish, too.

SERVES 4

SPECIAL EQUIPMENT:
> VACUUM SEALER (OPTIONAL)
> IMMERSION CIRCULATOR
> IMMERSION BLENDER

CALDEIRADA SAUCE

coriander seeds	1½ teaspoons
fennel seeds	1½ teaspoons
fresh parsley	4 sprigs
fresh thyme	2 sprigs
fresh bay leaf	½, notches torn every ½ inch (12 mm)
extra-virgin olive oil	as needed
white onions	1½, cut into ½-inch (12-mm) slices
fennel bulbs	1½, cored and cut into ½-inch (12-mm) slices, fronds reserved for garnish
garlic clove	1, minced
saffron threads	1½ teaspoons
dry white vinho verde	½ cup (120 ml)
Pernod	¼ cup (60 ml)
vine-ripened tomatoes	2, peeled, seeded, and cut into 1-inch (2.5-cm) dice (1½ cups/280 g)
pimentón (sweet smoked paprika)	pinch
Chicken Stock (page 226)	2 cups (480 ml), or as needed

VEGETABLES

extra-virgin olive oil	2 tablespoons
fennel bulb	1, cut into 1-inch (2.5-cm) batonettes
kosher salt	to taste
white onion	1, halved and cut into 1-inch- (2.5-cm-) thick slices
garlic cloves	4, sliced
saffron threads	pinch
Pernod	¼ cup (60 ml)
dry white vinho verde	½ cup (120 ml)
Chicken Stock (page 226)	2 cups (480 ml)
large Yukon gold potato	1, peeled and cut into ¼-inch (6-mm) cubes

FISH

skin-on red snapper	4 fillets (6 ounces/170 g each)
kosher salt and freshly ground white pepper	to taste
extra-virgin olive oil	2 tablespoons, plus more for serving
picked peekytoe crab meat	4 ounces (115 g)
fresh parsley leaves	1 tablespoon, finely chopped
fresh chives	1 tablespoon, thinly sliced
Dill Oil (page 239)	for serving

MAKE THE CALDEIRADA SAUCE: In a small skillet, heat the coriander and fennel seeds over medium heat, tossing occasionally, until toasted and fragrant. Transfer to a piece of cheesecloth along with the parsley, thyme, and bay leaf, and tie securely into a sachet.

Heat a 4-quart (3.8-L) saucepan over medium heat. Coat with oil, then add the onions, fennel bulb, garlic, and saffron. Sweat, stirring occasionally, until the vegetables are soft. Deglaze the pan with the vinho verde and Pernod, stirring until the liquid evaporates.

Add the tomatoes and cook, stirring occasionally, until they release their moisture and then become dry. Add the pimentón, then add the sachet and enough stock to just cover the mixture. Heat to a simmer and simmer, uncovered, for 30 minutes.

Discard the sachet. Transfer the mixture to a blender and puree until very smooth. Press the sauce through a fine-mesh sieve and return the liquid to the blender. With the machine running, add ¼ cup (60 ml) oil in a steady stream until emulsified.

MAKE THE VEGETABLES: Heat a 4-quart (3.8-L) rondeau (very large, wide, shallow pot) over medium-low heat. Add the oil, then the fennel. Season with salt and sweat, stirring occasionally, until just tender, about 5 minutes. Add the onion, garlic, saffron, and a pinch of salt. Sweat, stirring occasionally, until the onion is tender, about 10 minutes. Deglaze the pan with the Pernod, stirring until the liquid evaporates. Add the vinho verde and cook until the liquid evaporates. Add the stock, bring to a simmer, and adjust the heat to maintain a slow simmer for 10 minutes.

Meanwhile, in a small saucepan, cover the potato with cold water. Season generously with salt, heat to a simmer, and cook until tender. Drain and add to the vegetable mixture.

MAKE THE FISH: While the vegetables cook, score the skin sides of the snapper fillets with 4 diagonal slashes. Season 1 fillet on both sides with salt and pepper and place it in a heavy-duty ziptight plastic bag with 1½ teaspoons of the olive oil. Press out all the air and seal the bag tightly. Use a vacuum sealer if you have one. Repeat with each remaining fillet. Cook for 10 minutes in an immersion circulator set and held at 140°F (60°C).

After 8 minutes, gently heat the vegetables and the sauce if they've cooled. Stir 1 cup (240 ml) of the sauce into the vegetables. Remove the pan from the heat and fold in the crab, then the parsley and chives. Divide the mixture among four serving plates.

Remove the fish fillets from their bags and center on top of the vegetable mixture. Use an immersion blender to blend the remaining sauce until frothy and very smooth. Spoon the sauce around the fish and vegetables. Garnish with the reserved fennel fronds and drizzle a little dill oil and olive oil all around.

RED SNAPPER WITH SHELLFISH, TOMATO, AND SAFFRON

FESTIVAL FISH

1980 | VISEU

Every year, my family celebrated Dia de Portugal on June 10th with our local Portuguese-American club in Connecticut. We were a long way from Portugal, but the holiday is recognized by Portuguese all over the world. It commemorates the death of Luis de Camoes, our national poet, who chronicled the sixteenth-century conquests that made Portugal the reigning country of the world.

Centuries later, we're still celebrating. In my town, we'd set aside the Sunday closest to June 10th for a little parade around the block after mass. When we circled back to the church, we'd feast in the parking lot the way we did every saint's day and holiday. Folding tables and chairs crammed under a big tent, grills going with whole sardines blistering on the fire, music blaring from the speakers. It was fun running around with my cousins and friends, but I always passed on the sardines.

It took a trip across the Atlantic to get me to try our treasured national fish. I was eight when we stopped by an outdoor saint's-day festival in Portugal much like our church celebrations back home. My mom handed me a plate of sardines, just charred from the grill, and I decided to go for it. One bite and I was totally hooked. My family kept walking, but I parked myself at that sardine stand and polished off fish after fish, pulling the hot meat from the bones with my fingers.

When my mom realized I was missing, she freaked out . . . until she found me, fingers slick with olive oil, sardine heads and tails scattered around me as if some cat had gone to town. It remains one of her favorite memories and one of the earliest indications of what I might end up doing for a living. I like to believe that I knew the difference between the frozen sardines we got in Connecticut and the just-caught fish I had in Portugal. There's a huge difference, and I'm just glad that stores here now carry fresh ones, too.

GRILLED SARDINES WITH CHARRED PEPPERS

Fresh sardines are completely different from the tinny, salted canned kind. They're as fatty as salmon, but with firm yet flaky mild white flesh. Their thin skin's tough enough to hold up on the grill, but delicate—and delicious— enough to eat. I love the roasted, marinated peppers here, but the sardines are also great on their own with freshly squeezed lemon juice.

SERVES 2

poblano peppers	2
green bell pepper	1
red bell pepper	1
extra-virgin olive oil	as needed
kosher salt	to taste
sherry vinegar	to taste
sardines	6, gutted and cleaned
Maldon sea salt	to taste
fresh parsley leaves	1 tablespoon chopped
lemon wedges	4, for serving

Prepare a grill by heating a mixture of all-natural briquettes and hardwood lump charcoal until very hot.

Lightly coat the peppers with oil and very generously season with kosher salt. Place on the hot grill grate and grill, turning occasionally, until blackened and collapsed, about 15 minutes. Transfer to a dish. When they're cool enough to handle, peel the skins off and remove the stems and seeds. Cut the peppers into ½-inch- (12-mm-) wide strips and toss with oil and vinegar. Let stand to marinate.

Make sure your grill is still very hot. If not, add more charcoal and heat.

Lightly coat the sardines with oil and sprinkle generously with kosher salt. Place on the hot grill grate and grill, turning occasionally, until grill marks appear and the sardines start to whistle, about 8 minutes.

Transfer to serving plates and drizzle with oil. Sprinkle Maldon salt on top of the fish. Garnish with the parsley. Serve with the marinated peppers and lemon wedges.

TUNA WITH CUCUMBER, SMOKED PAPRIKA, AND VINHO VERDE

Even though there's an amazing amount of tuna off of Portugal's coast, it's not utilized much in the country's cuisine. I'm changing that here with this pure, simple sashimi-style preparation. I simply love this dish.

SERVES 4

extra-virgin olive oil	2 tablespoons
soy sauce	1 tablespoon
dry white vinho verde	1 tablespoon
yuzu or other citrus vinegar	2 teaspoons
pimentón (sweet smoked paprika)	½ teaspoon
grade A/1 big-eye tuna	5-by-3-inch/12-by-7.5-cm piece (8 ounces/224 g)
Kirby cucumber	1, peeled
shiso leaves	2, very thinly sliced
fresh thyme leaves	½ teaspoon
crushed red chile flakes	pinch

In a small bowl, whisk together the oil, soy sauce, vinho verde, vinegar, and pimentón. Cut the tuna into twenty 2-inch- (5-cm-) square, ¼-inch- (6-mm-) thick slices. Cut 20 slices of cucumber to the same size. Julienne the remaining cucumber. Arrange 5 slices of tuna on each of four serving plates and top with the cucumber. Whisk the dressing again and spoon all over, then garnish with the shiso, thyme, and chile flakes. Serve immediately.

SEA URCHIN TOASTS WITH SHISO AND LIME

On my days off, I eat sushi and sashimi more than anything else. I love Japanese food and this is my favorite way of treating sea urchin. The crunch of the toast, the briny sweetness of the sea urchin, and the heat of the mustard and wasabi are a great combination—it's so delicious.

Sea urchin "tongues" are shaped like tongues, but are actually the roe from inside the spiny sea creatures. I prefer the sweet large varieties harvested off the West Coast. Sometimes labeled uni, these delicacies are sold in specialty or Japanese fish markets and counters. They often come packaged in bamboo trays. Look for plump, bright-orange sea urchins that smell sweet and slightly briny.

SERVES 4

small cauliflower florets	½ cup (55 g)
whole milk	½ cup (120 ml)
kosher salt and freshly ground white pepper	to taste
extra-virgin olive oil	1 tablespoon, plus more as needed
baguette slices	4 (1½ by 2½ by ⅛ inch/ 4 by 6 cm by 3 mm)
Pickled Mustard Seeds (page 201)	2 teaspoons
freshly grated wasabi	2 teaspoons
West Coast sea urchin	12 tongues
mustard oil	to taste
soy sauce	to taste
lime	1
shiso leaf	1, very thinly sliced
Maldon sea salt	for serving

In a small saucepan, combine the cauliflower, milk, and a pinch of kosher salt. Bring to a simmer over high heat, then lower the heat, cover, and gently simmer until a cake tester pierces the cauliflower with no resistance.

Transfer the cauliflower mixture to a blender and puree until smooth. With the machine running, add the olive oil. Continue blending until emulsified. Press the puree through a fine-mesh sieve, season with kosher salt and pepper, and refrigerate until cold. Extra puree can be refrigerated for up to 3 days.

Preheat a broiler or salamander.

Rub the baguette slices with olive oil and toast until golden brown and crisp. On each toast, spread 1½ teaspoons cauliflower puree, leaving a ⅛-inch (3-mm) rim all around. Arrange three dots of mustard seeds on the puree, one dot on each end and one in the middle. Arrange three dots of wasabi next to the mustard dots. Align three sea urchin tongues on the baguette, tucking in their tapered ends. Very lightly drizzle the mustard oil, then the soy sauce over the sea urchin. Place the toasts on a baking sheet and warm them under the broiler for 30 seconds.

Zest the lime directly over the sea urchin, then cut the lime and squeeze a few drops of juice on top. Top with the shiso leaves and Maldon salt. Serve immediately.

CHAPTER 3

PORK: FRESH AND CURED

PORK BELLY AND CLAMS WITH PICKLES

CARNE DE PORCO ALENTEJANA

This is the one dish that fully represents Portuguese cooking and it is one of my favorites of all time. It's the epitome of the soulful meeting of land and sea. Briny clams, rich pork, earthy potatoes, sharp pickles, and savory olives end up being more than the sum of their parts. Seabra Marisqueria in Newark, New Jersey, has a killer preparation. This version's pretty great too.

SERVES 4

kosher salt	to taste
littleneck clams	24
golden nugget or other baby yellow potatoes	20, scrubbed
extra-virgin olive oil	as needed
Refogado (page 235)	¼ cup (60 ml)
garlic cloves	4, crushed
fresh bay leaves	2, notches torn every ½ inch (12 mm)
fresh thyme	4 sprigs
dry white vinho verde	4 cups (960 ml), plus more as needed
Pork Jus (page 230)	½ cup (120 ml)
Roasted Pork Belly (page 96)	2 pieces (½ recipe), cut into 1-inch (2.5-cm) cubes
Cauliflower and Carrot Pickles (page 201)	5 each, cut into small pieces
pitted kalamata olives	¼ cup (35 g), cut into ¼-inch (6-mm) slices
fresh parsley leaves	2 tablespoons, finely chopped
fresh cilantro leaves	2 tablespoons, finely chopped

Fill a bowl with cold water and dissolve enough salt in it to make it taste like the ocean. Submerge the clams in the water. Let them sit for 10 minutes or until they spit out their grit. You should see sand at the bottom of the bowl. Lift out the clams and transfer to a colander. With a stiff-bristled brush, scrub them vigorously until their shells are really clean.

Bring a large saucepan of water to a boil and very generously salt it. Add the potatoes and cook until tender. A cake tester should slide through a potato easily. Drain and cool, then cut each in half.

Fill a small saucepan with oil to a depth of 2 inches (5 cm). Heat to 350°F (175°C). Add a few of the potato halves and cook, turning occasionally, until browned and crisp, about 5 minutes. Drain on paper towels. Repeat with the remaining potatoes.

Heat a large saucepan over medium heat and coat with oil. Add the refogado, garlic, bay leaves, and thyme and cook, stirring, until fragrant, about 30 seconds. Add the clams, stir to coat with the aromatics, then add the vinho verde. The wine should come halfway up the clams; add more if needed. Bring to a boil, cover, and cook until the clams start to open. Pull the clams out as they open and transfer to a dish. Start checking after 1 minute, covering the pan again after each time you check; they should all be open within 5 minutes. Discard any that are not. Drizzle the clams with oil.

Let the sauce remaining in the pan boil for 2 minutes. Discard the bay leaves and thyme, then stir in the pork jus. Keep warm over low heat.

Heat a large, deep skillet over high heat. Add just enough oil to coat the bottom of the pan, then add the pork in a single layer. Work in batches if necessary. Cook, turning to evenly brown all sides, until golden brown, about 30 seconds per side. If working in batches, transfer to a plate and repeat with the remaining pork.

Return all the pork to the skillet and add the clam cooking liquid. Reduce the heat to low and add the clams and potatoes. Carefully toss to evenly coat and glaze everything. Remove from the heat and top with the pickles, olives, parsley, and cilantro. Serve immediately.

PORK BELLY AND CLAMS WITH PICKLES

MARINATED GRILLED PORK TENDERLOIN

My mom's go-to marinade for meat is dead simple and delicious. Even though there's only a splash of vinho verde, the aromas of the wine really come through the smoky char of the meat.

SERVES 4

extra-virgin olive oil	¼ cup (60 ml), plus more as needed
dry white vinho verde	2 tablespoons
fresh thyme	4 sprigs
fresh bay leaf	1, thinly sliced at an angle
crushed red chile flakes	½ teaspoon
pimentón (smoked sweet paprika)	½ teaspoon
pork tenderloin	1 whole (¾ pound/340 g)
kosher salt	to taste

In a large dish, whisk together the oil, vinho verde, thyme, bay leaf, chile flakes, and pimentón. Cut the pork into 1½-inch- (3.75-cm-) thick steaks at a 45-degree angle. Cutting the meat on the bias helps keep it tender. Add the meat to the marinade and turn well to coat. Cover and refrigerate for 3 to 5 hours.

When you're ready to cook, prepare a grill by heating a mixture of all-natural briquettes and hardwood lump charcoal to medium-high heat. Take the pork out of the marinade, picking off the herbs, and transfer the marinade to a small saucepan. Bring the marinade to a boil and boil for 5 minutes. The mixture will look broken. Remove from the heat.

Season the pork generously with salt and drizzle with oil. Grill until charred, flip, and char the other side, about 5 minutes. Flip again, brush on some of the cooked marinade and cook for 2 to 3 minutes more, then repeat with the other side. Grill until the pork is still a little pink in the center, 10 to 12 minutes total.

Spoon any remaining cooked marinade over the pork and let rest for a few minutes before serving.

CURED PORK LOIN

Over the past few years, I've been playing with different pork-curing techniques and this one strikes the right balance between smoky and fresh flavors.

SERVES 12

SPECIAL EQUIPMENT:
> SMOKER

coriander seeds	1 tablespoon
juniper berries	1 tablespoon
kosher salt	2¾ cups (685 g)
sugar	1¼ cups (250 g)
pink curing salt	¼ cup (65 g)
boneless center-cut pork loin	1 whole (5 to 5½ pounds/2.3 to 2.5 kg)
Pickles (page 200)	for serving
good mustard	for serving

In a small skillet, heat the coriander and juniper over medium heat, tossing occasionally, until toasted and fragrant. Cool completely, then lightly crush and combine with the kosher salt, sugar, and pink salt.

Butterfly the pork loin by cutting a deep slit lengthwise down the center. Don't cut all the way through; leave 1½ inches (4 cm) uncut meat on the bottom. Cut two more slits lengthwise on the cut sides, again leaving 1½ inches (4 cm) uncut. Open the loin like a book. Place the pork in a pan that can fit it snugly and completely cover with the salt mixture. Cover tightly with plastic wrap and refrigerate overnight.

Prepare a smoker to maintain an even low heat and scatter with wood chips, preferably applewood chips.

Uncover the pork, rinse off the salt mixture, and pat very dry. Roll into its loin shape and tie very tightly with kitchen twine at 1-inch (2.5-cm) intervals. Smoke until burnished and fragrant, about 30 minutes.

Transfer the loin to a piece of cheesecloth, wrap tightly and secure with kitchen twine, then wrap in foil. Prepare a large steamer. I use a hotel pan with a perforated pan insert. If your steamer can't fit the whole loin, cut the loin into pieces that will fit your steamer and wrap each piece individually in cheesecloth and foil. Steam the pork over gently simmering water until a meat thermometer registers 145°F (62°C) when inserted into the thickest part of the loin.

Remove the loin from the steamer and discard the foil. Let the pork rest at room temperature for 30 minutes. If you have room to hang the loin in your refrigerator, tie long pieces of kitchen twine on both ends of the cheesecloth and hang it with a dish underneath. Otherwise, place the pork on a wire rack set in a pan. Refrigerate for 5 to 7 days to let the flavors mature.

When you're ready to serve, cut the pork into thin slices and serve with pickles and mustard. And lots of cold beer.

THE SEARCH FOR SUCKLING PIG

2013 | AGUEDA

You know you're heading to the middle of nowhere when your smartphone GPS flashes "no location found" after you've typed in the name of the village. Even the printed road map doesn't show it. I'm looking for Casa Vidal, supposedly home of the best leitão (roast suckling pig) in the central Beira region. I'm wondering if I'll ever get there. It's only in retrospect, of course, that I realize how the journey to good pork showed me the soul of Portugal.

Before I even hit the highway, I call Casa Vidal to ask what time they close for lunch. The woman sweetly replies, "2 p.m." That gives me an hour to get there, exactly what I need. From Porto, I race down the highway, then pull off at the sign for Agueda, the nearest large town, and come to a dead stop. A line of trucks huff gray smoke on this single-lane road snaking through industrial parks. Maybe these factories are a sign of progress, but the infrastructure clearly hasn't caught up.

I veer onto a side road while Genevieve tries to reroute us on the phone and figure out where we are on the road map. As suddenly as we hit that stretch of industry, we end up in the rotary of a town quaint enough to be a movie set. And it feels as surreal as a Fellini film. All along the main strip, hundreds of open umbrellas—bright red, blue, orange, yellow—are strung between the wrought-iron balconies. With the breeze, they move like a wave over the lampposts and café tables below. And they're a clear sign that we're lost.

Now that it's five minutes to 2 p.m., Genevieve calls the restaurant to let them know we'll be late and to ask for directions, but she can't get past "hello" in Portuguese. I grab the phone with my right hand and steer around and around the rotary with my left. As a New Yorker, I expect them to say, "Too bad. We're closed. Better luck next time." Instead, she promises to save us a platter of suckling pig and tells us which way to go from the rotary. And she says she's sending a driver from the restaurant to direct us from the next big intersection. That's hospitality.

Along the way, the landscape continues shifting, going from car dealerships to crumbling stone churches. It all feels stuck in time, albeit in different eras. When I spot the panel van with the logo of an impaled piglet, I follow. We circle nameless roads until we pull up to a neat white building. I had expected a roadhouse, all rough-hewn beams and sawdust floors. Instead, the glass doors open to a marble entryway with dark wood paneling and a vase of orchids. In the white-tablecloth dining room, a tile mural of the original owner sliding a pig into a wood oven serves as decor.

Even though the servers are now sitting down to their staff meal before dinner, they graciously bring the leitão they saved for us. And it's crazy good. Smoky, garlicky, moist, tender. It's all I want in roasted pork. What makes it exceptional is the generosity of the staff making and serving it. These people have no idea I'm visiting as an American chef researching a cookbook. I'm just another guy and they saved me food, kept the dining room open, sent a driver to lead me to the place, and now, after all that, José Vidal, the second-generation owner, offers to show me their whole operation.

We start all the way in the back, where piglets born on a farm a few miles away shuffle around a hay-strewn pen. They're dinner. We pass the spotless room where veterinarians oversee the quick and humane slaughtering, then enter the work station where cooks mix a pungent garlic marinade. Without my asking, José offers to demonstrate how to properly roast leitão. A server starts throwing logs into the wood oven while José slips on gloves and starts rubbing the marinade into a piglet. Together, they slide a pole through the piglet and tie it on tightly before hoisting it into the oven. When the skin burnishes to a deep brown, the piglet's cut into hunks, bones and all. Each platter features all parts of the piglet, so beneath each bite of smoky, crackling skin, each diner gets a variety of fatty, meaty textures. José's technique is the same as the one used the day his parents opened the restaurant in 1964 and for generations before that, too.

The dining room may be air-conditioned and the cooking facilities sparkling enough to shock the most jaded health inspector, but the food remains unchanged. I'm not sure I could've appreciated Casa Vidal's preservation of the art of leitão had I not seen the real Portugal—the less-than-picturesque evolution of the country from centuries-old churches to mid-century factories—along the way. I certainly wouldn't have experienced the full extent of their hospitality, a tradition as deep as the leitão itself.

Top: The wood-burning oven at Casa Vidal.
Bottom: Casa Vidal's plate of suckling pig comes with a variety of cuts.

ROAST SUCKLING PIG

LEITÃO

The meat and fat of young suckling pigs is unbelievably delicious. It's so tender it melts in your mouth. When you roast it whole, the skin caramelizes into a crisp shell. Because the meat itself tastes so good, I simply rub it with the classic Portuguese garlic-vinegar marinade and then serve it with Iceberg, Cucumber, and Tomato Salad (page 144) and potatoes (see pages 195–196). Be sure to call your butcher at least a week ahead of time to special order a whole suckling pig. You can also ask them to butterfly the pig for you.

SERVES 8 TO 10

garlic	6 heads, cloves peeled and minced
extra-virgin olive oil	1 cup (240 ml)
white vinegar	½ cup (120 ml)
coarse sea salt	2 tablespoons
crushed black peppercorns	2 tablespoons
suckling pig	1 whole (8 to 12 pounds/3.6 to 5.4 kg)

Preheat the oven to 425°F (220°C). Fit a wire rack into a half sheet pan.

In a medium bowl, whisk together the garlic, oil, vinegar, salt, and pepper until emulsified. Using a very sharp knife, spatchcock the pig by cutting through the belly from end to end, leaving the back intact. You should be able to open the pig so that it looks like it's flying. Rub the garlic paste all over the inside of the pig, getting it into the legs and shoulders.

Place the pig on the rack in the pan, skin-side up. Cover the ears with foil. Roast for 45 minutes, then reduce the heat to 350°F (175°C). Continue roasting until a cake tester inserted in the thickest part of the leg feels warm (the internal temperature should register 145°F/60°C), 15 to 20 minutes.

Transfer the pig to a large cutting board and tent with foil to rest for 20 minutes. With a sharp knife, cut off the legs, shoulders, and belly. Use kitchen shears to cut the meat into serving pieces.

PIG'S TROTTERS TERRINE

One thing I learned from culinary school and working with the French masters is the importance of classic, focused technique. Case in point: how to make a perfectly clear stock. Egg whites help pull all the impurities out of the liquid. The beautiful golden stock you get here would be just as delicious in any soup or even drunk alone, and its high natural gelatin content makes it perfect for binding this terrine together.

SERVES 12

fresh lemon thyme	3 sprigs, plus ¾ teaspoon leaves
whole black peppercorns	1 tablespoon
coriander seeds	1 tablespoon
pig's trotters	2 whole ham hocks with shoulders attached or 2 trotters and 2 shanks
Pork Stock (page 228)	1 quart (960 ml), plus more as needed
dry white vinho verde	1 cup (240 ml)
garlic cloves	2
carrots	2 medium, peeled and chopped
white onions	2 small, chopped
celery stalks	2 small, chopped
kosher salt	to taste
tomato paste	1½ teaspoons
egg whites	7 large

Wrap the thyme sprigs, peppercorns, and coriander in cheesecloth, then tie them securely into a sachet. Transfer to a large saucepot with the pig's hocks or trotters and shanks, stock, vinho verde, garlic, half of the carrots, onions, and celery, and a generous pinch of salt. The liquid should come two-thirds of the way up the solids. If necessary, add more stock.

Bring to a simmer over high heat, then reduce the heat to maintain a low bubble. Simmer, skimming the foam that rises to the surface, until the meat falls off the bones, 2 to 3 hours. Transfer the meat to a dish. Strain the cooking liquid through a fine-mesh sieve and refrigerate until cold. When the meat is cool enough to handle, pull it and a little of the fat off the bones. Refrigerate the meat until ready to use; discard the bones.

Combine the tomato paste with the remaining carrots, onions, and celery in a food processor. Puree until almost smooth. Transfer to a saucepot with the chilled cooking liquid. Whisk the egg whites in a bowl until frothy and add to the pot. Bring to a simmer over medium heat. A raft of the solids will begin to form on the surface. Once the raft is fully formed, make a 2-inch- (5-cm-) round opening in the top with a spoon. Adjust the heat to maintain a low bubble for 30 minutes.

Line a fine-mesh sieve with cheesecloth and set over a large bowl. Carefully ladle the liquid through the raft into the sieve. Don't break the raft; if you do, the liquid will get cloudy. The strained liquid should be golden and clear. Season with salt, then refrigerate until cold. When chilled, skim the fat from the surface of the liquid and discard it.

Line an 8-by-4-inch (20-by-10-cm) loaf pan with plastic wrap, leaving overhang on all four sides. Ladle in enough of the liquid to come ¼ inch (6 mm) up the sides. Arrange a single layer of the trotter meat pieces, overlapping them slightly so that there are no gaps. Ladle in enough liquid to just cover the meat, then add another layer of meat and sprinkle with ¼ teaspoon lemon thyme leaves. Repeat the layering until the meat and thyme are used up. Gently press the final layer of meat flat with your fingers, then add enough liquid to just cover the meat and thyme leaves. Fold the plastic wrap overhang over the mixture to completely cover. Set the pan on a rimmed baking dish. Set another 8-by-4-inch (20-by-10-cm) loaf pan on top of the terrine and place 2 to 3 pounds (896 g to 1.4kg) of weights in the top pan. Refrigerate at least overnight for up to 7 days.

When you're ready to serve, remove the top pan with weights, uncover the top of the terrine, invert onto a serving platter, and discard the plastic wrap. Slice the terrine and serve it cold.

CRISPY PIGS' EARS WITH RAMPS AND CUMIN YOGURT

When fried, pigs' ears become as crisp as chips with an added layer of porkiness. We knew we wanted them on Aldea's menu when we opened in 2009. Since it was spring, we served them with bright spring ramps, both sautéed and pickled, to cut through their richness.

SERVES 4

SPECIAL EQUIPMENT:
> PRESSURE COOKER

pigs' ears	8 ounces (225 g)
white onion	¼ small, chopped
carrot	¼ small, peeled and chopped
celery stalk	½ small, chopped
garlic cloves	3 whole
fresh bay leaf	1, notches torn every ½ inch (12 mm)
whole black peppercorns	½ teaspoon
fresh thyme	1 sprig
kosher salt and freshly ground white pepper	to taste
cumin seeds	¾ teaspoon
plain whole-milk Greek yogurt	¼ cup (60 ml)
canola oil	as needed
extra-virgin olive oil	as needed
ramp leaves	4 cups (4 ounces/112 g)
Ramp Bulb Pickles (page 201)	16
sweet-tart apple	½ small, cored and thinly sliced
fresh chives	2 tablespoons thinly sliced
fresh lime juice	to taste

Combine the pigs' ears, onion, carrot, celery, garlic, bay leaf, peppercorns, thyme, and ½ teaspoon salt in a pressure cooker. Add enough cold water to cover by 1 inch (2.5 cm). Secure the pressure cooker according to the manufacturer's instructions and simmer until the cartilage in the ears is soft, 3 to 4 hours. The ears should be gelatinous. Let the ears cool to room temperature in the liquid, then remove them from the liquid and pat dry. Cut into very thin slices.

Meanwhile, in a small skillet, heat the cumin over medium heat, tossing occasionally, until toasted and fragrant. Let cool completely, then pulse in a spice grinder until finely ground. Stir into the yogurt and season with salt.

Fill a small saucepan with canola oil to a depth of 2 inches (5 cm). Bring to 350°F (175°C) over medium-high heat. Carefully drop a few ear slices into the oil. Don't crowd the pan; fry a few at a time. Fry, adjusting the heat to maintain the temperature, until crisp, about 7 minutes. Drain on paper towels. Repeat with the remaining ears.

Heat a large skillet over medium-high heat. Add enough olive oil to coat the bottom, then add the ramps and season with salt. Cook, stirring occasionally, until wilted and bright green.

Divide the yogurt among four serving plates and top with the ramp leaves, pigs' ears, pickled ramps, apple, and chives. Drizzle with lime juice and olive oil and season with salt and pepper.

ROASTED PORK BELLY

The pork shoulder's the cut traditionally roasted in Portugal, but I prefer the tender, fatty, juicy belly. Despite the richness of the meat, it can actually be overcooked, so be sure to test it periodically. This brined belly is definitely good enough to eat on its own, but it tastes even better when thrown into a skillet with clams (page 82).

SERVES 20

whole cloves	12
whole star anise	5
cinnamon sticks	2
whole white peppercorns	2 tablespoons
fennel seeds	1 tablespoon
coriander seeds	1 tablespoon
fresh bay leaves	5, notches torn every ½ inch (12 mm)
sugar	4 cups (800 g)
kosher salt	4 cups (1 kg)
boneless, skin-on pork belly	1 whole slab (9 pounds/4 kg), cut in quarters

In a large saucepan, combine the cloves, star anise, cinnamon, peppercorns, fennel seeds, and coriander. Heat over medium heat, shaking the pan occasionally, until fragrant and toasted. Stir in the bay leaves, sugar, salt, and 3 quarts (2.8 L) water just until the sugar and salt dissolve. Remove from heat and let cool completely.

Divide the pork belly and brine between two large zip-tight plastic bags. Seal tightly and refrigerate overnight.

Preheat the oven to 350°F (175°C). Set a wire rack in a roasting pan.

Remove the pork from the brine, rinse, and pat dry. Place on the wire rack, fat-side up, and roast until golden brown and tender, 3 to 4 hours. The pork should still hold its shape and a cake tester or thin paring knife should slide through easily.

Serve on its own or use it in other recipes. If you want it in even slices or chunks for another recipe, it's easier to cut when cold, so refrigerate first until firm.

VARIATION

SOUS-VIDE If you have sous-vide equipment (a vacuum machine or food saver and an immersion circulator), cryovac the pork with the brine in two bags. Sous-vide at 162°F (72°C) for 36 hours. Remove the pork from the bag and brine, picking off any spices stuck to the meat.

BRAISED PORK BELLY

cinnamon stick	1
whole star anise	1
whole black peppercorns	2 teaspoons
coriander seeds	2 teaspoons
rendered bacon fat	1 teaspoon
boneless, skin-on pork belly	1 pound (455 g), cut into 6-inch- (15-cm-) square pieces
kosher salt	to taste
carrot	1 small, peeled and thinly sliced
celery stalk	½ rib, very thinly sliced at an angle
white onion	1 small, sliced
garlic cloves	3, sliced
fresh thyme	3 sprigs
fresh rosemary	1 sprig
fresh bay leaf	1, notches torn every ½ inch (12 mm)
dry white vinho verde	1 cup (240 ml)
pimentón (sweet smoked paprika)	1½ teaspoons
Pork Stock (page 228)	1 cup (240 ml), or as needed

The whole spices in the simmering stock here penetrate the fatty pork, while the combination of bacon fat and pimentón brings smokiness to this stovetop braise. The meat can then be eaten tender as is or fried crisp, as in the Spiced Pork Belly Cracklins (page 98). Either way, it's delicious.

SERVES 4

In a small skillet, heat the cinnamon, star anise, peppercorns, and coriander over medium heat, tossing occasionally, until toasted and fragrant.

In a medium Dutch oven or casserole, heat the bacon fat over medium-high heat until it melts. Season the pork belly with salt and add to the pan, fat-side down. Cook until golden brown and caramelized, about 5 minutes. Pour out excess fat from the pan and reserve. Turn the pork belly over and cook until the meat side is golden, about 3 minutes, then turn and cook the sides until golden, about 1 minute each. Transfer the belly to a plate and pour out all but a thin layer of fat from the pan into the reserved fat. The browning here creates great flavors; it's a crucial first step.

Add the carrot, celery, onion, and garlic to the pan and season with salt. Stir well, adding some of the reserved fat back to the pan if the mixture looks dry. Cook, stirring occasionally, until crisp-tender, about 2 minutes, then add the thyme, rosemary, bay leaf, and toasted spices. Again, add fat if the mixture looks dry. Cook, stirring, for about 1 minute.

Stir in the vinho verde and pimentón. Bring the mixture to a boil and boil until the liquid is reduced by half. Return the belly to the pan, skin-side up, and set on top of the vegetables. Add enough stock to come halfway up the pork. Bring the mixture to a simmer, cover, and simmer for 30 minutes. Flip the pork over and simmer until tender but still holding its shape, another 1½ hours.

Transfer the pork to a serving dish. Strain the cooking liquid over the pork and serve. If making ahead or using for Spiced Pork Belly Cracklins (page 98), refrigerate the meat and cooking liquid separately until cold, at least 3 hours or for up to 1 day ahead.

SPICED PORK BELLY CRACKLINS

This is not what I'd call a healthy snack. But it's a damn good one. If you happen to have my Goan Spice Mix (page 233) on hand, sprinkle a pinch on just before serving.

SERVES 4

Braised Pork Belly (page 97) 1 recipe pork plus cooking liquid, chilled
sherry vinegar 1 teaspoon
canola oil as needed

Cut the pork belly into 1-by-½-by-½-inch (2.5-cm-by-12-by-12-mm) rectangular pieces. Scrape the fat off the cooking liquid and discard. Bring the cooking liquid to a boil and simmer until reduced to a syrupy consistency. Remove from the heat and stir in the vinegar.

Meanwhile, fill a small saucepan with oil to a depth of 3 inches (7.5 cm). Heat to 375°F (190°C). Add a few pieces of the pork belly and cook, turning occasionally, until evenly browned, 3 to 5 minutes. There's a lot of fat in the belly, so it takes some time for the pieces to really crisp up. Drain on paper towels and repeat with the remaining belly. Toss in the sauce and serve immediately.

FOR THE LOVE OF HAM

PORTUGAL TO CONNECTICUT, SPAIN TO TENNESSEE

Even though I was born in Danbury, Connecticut, I might as well have been raised in Ferreirós do Dão, my family's village in the central beira alta region of Portugal. When the economy there hit an especially rough patch and the U.S. Government opened its doors to immigrants in 1965, my parents' generation transplanted themselves. From the hillside river village, they trickled into Danbury to work in the factories and build better lives for my generation.

When I returned to Ferreirós do Dão to further research this book, I revisited the plaque bearing the poem my grandfather wrote in 1977 in honor of the village. And sitting on the stone benches beneath was a man from the block where I grew up. In fact, everyone I met in Ferreirós do Dão remembered me and my parents. I even got to chat with the ninety-year-old woman who lived across the way from my grandmother's old home in the village. She still recalled the summers I spent playing with my sister on the gravel path outside her front door and the years she spent caring for my ill grandmother before she passed.

Each time I head down the eucalyptus-lined road to the village, I feel the same instinctive "going home" sensation I get when I cross the Connecticut state line on I-84. As a kid, I never felt as American as the rugby shirt–wearing blue bloods at my school. (I was all about the mullet and bolo ties.) And when I stopped for directions in Portugal, the man immediately asked, "Americano?" But I'm comfortable in both cultures and consider myself lucky to have two distinct culinary heritages.

CASE IN POINT: HAM

One of my favorite hams is not actually from Portugal, but from its neighbor Spain. (But my favorite place to eat it is in Lisbon, hand-sliced at the bar of Cervejaria Ramiro.) Pata Negra Cinco Jotas from Sanchez Romero Carvajal comes from Iberian black pigs raised in Jabugo, in a park near Seville that UNESCO declared a "Biosphere Reserve." The pure-bred pigs roam the expansive grounds for their feed of acorns, beans, herbs, and wildflowers that give them a distinctive nutty aroma. Salted, then cured for at least three years, both the meat and fat become silky, delicate, and punishingly delicious.

On this side of the Atlantic, I love Benton's Smoky Mountain Country Hams (and his bacon, too) from Madisonville, Tennessee. My friend Sean Brock, a chef in Charleston, South Carolina, introduced me to Allan Benton's products. Like Cinco Jotas's pata negra, the pigs—although a different breed—are just as carefully raised. The other big difference: sugar. Brown sugar is part of Benton's salt cure and the hams, some of which are also hickory-smoked, are aged for about a year. The texture's meaty, the flavor intense.

Tasting those two hams will give you a sense of where my dual cultures converge. The companies share a commitment to sustainable slow-food production and upholding long-standing culinary traditions. Even though their tastes are distinct, both products represent the best of cured pork and what I love about being both Portuguese and American.

EGGS BAKED WITH PEAS, LINGUIÇA, AND BACON

OVOS ESCALFADOS COM
ERVILHAS E LINGUIÇA

All the porkiness here—it's as Portuguese as you're gonna get. To add a little freshness to the original, I finish the dish with parsley and lemon. It's still hearty enough to make this the sort of warming dish I want to eat in a Vermont cabin after skiing.

SERVES 4

extra-virgin olive oil	as needed
smoked slab bacon, preferably Benton's	1½ ounces (40 g), cut into ½-inch (12-mm) slices, then into ½-inch (12-mm) batons
white onion	½ medium, finely diced
garlic cloves	3, thinly sliced
fresh bay leaf	1, notches torn every ½ inch (12 mm)
crushed red chile flakes	pinch
strained tomatoes	3 tablespoons
linguiça	2 ounces (55 g), cut into ½-inch (12-mm) dice
chouriço	¾ ounce (20 g), casing removed, thinly sliced
peas	2 cups (240 g) thawed frozen
kosher salt	to taste
eggs	4 large
fresh parsley leaves	¼ cup (7 g), chopped
fresh lemon juice	to taste

Preheat the oven to 350°F (175°C).

Heat a 4-quart (3.8-L) cast-iron cocotte or Dutch oven over medium heat. Add just enough oil to coat the bottom, then add the bacon. Cook, stirring occasionally, until the fat is rendered and the bacon is lightly browned, about 4 minutes. Transfer the bacon to a dish.

Add the onion, garlic, bay leaf, and chile flakes to the cocotte and cook, stirring, until the onion is tender but not browned, about 3 minutes. Add the tomatoes and 1 teaspoon oil and cook, stirring and scraping down the sides of the pan, for 4 minutes. The tomatoes should be sizzling steadily. Stir in the linguiça, chouriço, reserved bacon, and 1 teaspoon more oil. Cook, stirring occasionally, until heated through, about 2 minutes. Stir in the peas and season with salt. Discard the bay leaf.

Make four little nests for the eggs in the mixture, spacing them a few inches apart. Carefully break an egg into each nest, making sure each one is nestled in the stew and flush with the top.

Bake until the egg whites are set but the yolks are still runny, about 8 minutes. Top with the parsley and season with the lemon juice. Serve immediately.

LINGUIÇA, CHOURIÇO, AND PARSLEY OMELET

Also known as mom's feel-good omelet. On Sundays, we'd have our big family meal early in the day, so she'd throw this snack together late in the afternoon. Leftovers turned into sandwiches for my dad's lunch box. No matter how you eat it, it's comfort food at its best.

SERVES 2

eggs	5 large
extra-virgin olive oil	1½ tablespoons
linguiça	1½ ounces (40 g), cut into ⅛-inch (3-mm) slices
chouriço	1½ ounces (40 g), casing removed, cut into ⅛-inch (3-mm) slices
fresh parsley leaves	¼ cup (7 g), very finely chopped
kosher salt	to taste

In a medium bowl, beat the eggs with a fork until well blended.

Heat a large nonstick skillet over medium heat. Add ½ tablespoon of the oil and heat, then add the linguiça and chouriço. Cook, stirring occasionally, until the fat is rendered and the edges of the linguiça curl up a bit and lightly brown, about 2 minutes. Drain the sausages on paper towels and wipe out the pan.

Heat the pan over medium heat and add the remaining 1 tablespoon oil. Return the sausages to the pan, then add the eggs. Scatter the parsley over the wet eggs. Run a rubber spatula around the edges of the pan to lift the set parts of the egg and let the wet eggs run under. Repeat until the eggs are just set but still wet. Season with salt.

With the rubber spatula, carefully fold over one-third of the eggs, then fold again to make a 3-roll omelet. Tip out of the pan. Serve immediately, warm, or at room temperature, cutting into slices if you want. This is great with simple garden greens lightly dressed in a sherry vinaigrette.

FRIED EGGS WITH CHANTERELLES, MORCELLA, AND POTATOES

Bring the big frying pan of crisp sausage and eggs, sautéed mushrooms, and creamy potatoes to the table for everyone to dig into. The runny yolks become this amazing "sauce" that binds all the flavors and textures together.

SERVES 4

extra-virgin olive oil	as needed
morcella (blood) sausage (see Note)	6 ounces (170 g), cut into ½-inch- (12-mm-) thick half-moons
girolles (baby chanterelles)	1 cup (55 g), trimmed
fresh thyme	2 sprigs, plus ½ teaspoon leaves
Potatoes Confit (page 195)	20, quartered
lemon wedges	to taste
fresh parsley leaves	1 teaspoon, finely chopped
eggs	4 large
kosher salt and freshly ground black pepper	to taste

Heat a large skillet over medium-high heat and lightly coat the bottom with oil. Add the morcella and cook, stirring and shaking the pan occasionally, until golden brown, about 3 minutes. Carefully drain the fat from the pan, then add the mushrooms and thyme sprigs. Cook, stirring, until the mushrooms are brown, about 2 minutes. Toss in the potatoes and cook, stirring, until heated through. Remove from the heat, discard the thyme sprigs, and squirt lemon juice on top to taste. Sprinkle with the parsley and thyme leaves. The morcella will make the mixture salty, but season with salt if you feel it's needed.

Meanwhile, heat a large frying pan over medium-high heat. Add enough oil to generously coat the bottom and heat until hot. Add the eggs, season with salt and pepper, and cook until the whites are brown and crisp around the edges. Tilt the pan slightly and spoon the hot oil over the tops of the eggs to almost finish cooking the whites. Don't let the yolks set; they should stay runny. Remove from the heat and serve immediately on top of the sausage-potato mixture.

NOTE *Morcella, or blood sausage, has an intense, deep flavor. You can find Portuguese varieties in Latin or specialty meat markets. You can also try this dish with other sausages or even bacon.*

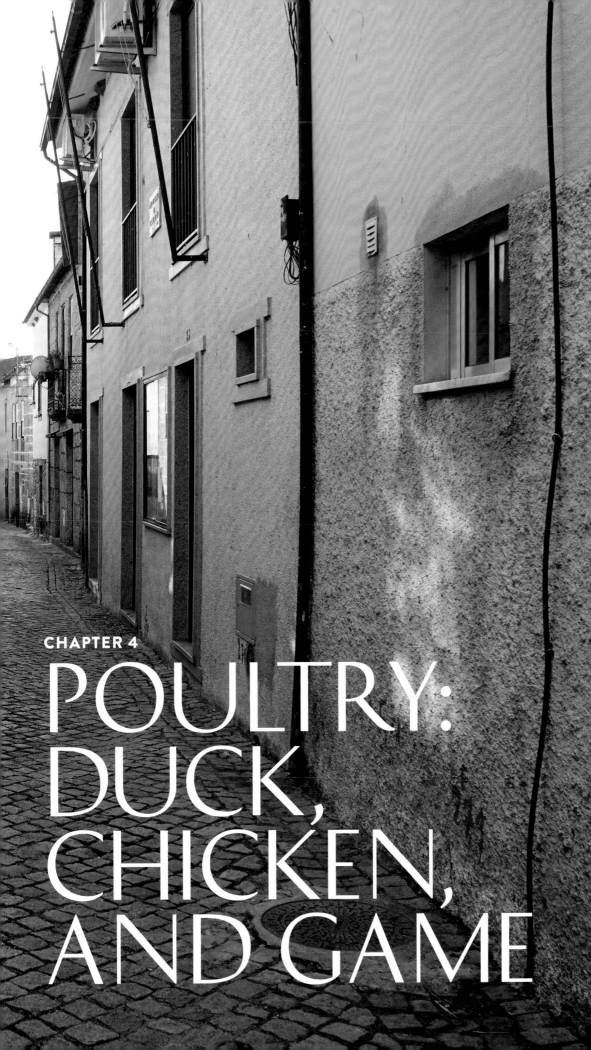

CHAPTER 4

POULTRY: DUCK, CHICKEN, AND GAME

DUCK RICE

If there's one dish that defines the flavors of my childhood and of Aldea, this is it. And it all started with my mom. She prepares great Portuguese rice dishes and I wanted to pay respect to her and my ancestors by making a traditional dish my own for my restaurant. With this classic one-pot duck rice, I zoomed in on the ingredients, amplified their flavors, and presented it in a totally new way. I took my French training and deconstructed the duck: confited the legs to fold into rich calasparra rice toasted with refogado, made stock and jus from the bones to flavor the whole thing, cooked the breast sous-vide to arrange its rare slices on top, and fashioned crisp, savory cracklins from the skin as a finishing touch. I included chouriço and olives for good measure and made sure the rice developed its own crust too. It's simply wholesome and warming, but also complex with its satisfying depth of flavor and contrasting textures. It's the definition of refined rusticity.

SERVES 6 TO 8

SPECIAL EQUIPMENT:
> VACUUM SEALER
> IMMERSION CIRCULATOR

DUCK CONFIT

Long Island (Pekin) ducks	2 whole (4 to 4½ pounds / 1.8 to 2 kg each)
fresh thyme	4 sprigs
fresh rosemary	1 sprig
fresh bay leaf	1, notches torn every ½ inch (12 mm)
duck fat	3 cups (720 ml)
kosher salt and freshly ground white pepper	to taste
white onion	1 cup (120 g) diced
carrot	1, peeled and sliced
celery stalk	1, sliced
garlic cloves	3, sliced
coriander seeds	1 tablespoon
whole white peppercorns	1 tablespoon
whole star anise	2

DUCK STOCK

canola oil	2 tablespoons
kosher salt	as needed
white onion	1 cup (120 g) chopped
celery	½ cup (50 g) sliced
carrot	½ cup (65 g) sliced
tomato paste	1 tablespoon

DUCK JUS

extra-virgin olive oil	2 tablespoons
kosher salt	as needed
white onion	½, cut into 1-inch (2.5-cm) slices
celery stalk	1, cut into ½-inch (12-mm) slices
carrot	½, peeled and cut into ½-inch (12-mm) slices
garlic cloves	3, crushed
tomato paste	1 tablespoon

MAKE THE CONFIT: Cut off the duck legs and reserve. Cut the breast halves off the bones and reserve; remove the skins and use them to make Duck Skin Cracklins (page 112). Cut the carcass into 2-inch (5-cm) pieces and reserve, along with the necks.

Preheat the oven to 300°F (150°C). Wrap the thyme, rosemary, and bay leaf in cheesecloth, then tie securely into a sachet.

Heat a small roasting pan over medium-high heat and melt 1 tablespoon of the duck fat in it. Season the duck legs generously with salt and pepper, then add to the pan. Sear, turning occasionally, until golden brown. Transfer to a plate.

Add the onion, carrot, celery, garlic, and a pinch of salt to the pan. Sweat, stirring occasionally, until tender. Add the coriander, peppercorns, star anise, and herb sachet. Cook, stirring occasionally, for 5 minutes. Add the remaining duck fat, melt, and bring to a slow bubble. Return the duck legs to the pan, submerging them in the mixture, and cover tightly with foil.

Bake until the meat falls off the bones, 6 to 8 hours. Remove the duck from the pan. When cool enough to handle, pull the meat off the bones in long ½-inch- (12-mm-) wide pieces. Discard the bones and cartilage. Strain the duck fat and reserve for future use. The duck legs can be stored in the fat for up to 5 days.

MAKE THE STOCK: Preheat the oven to 400°F (205°C) with a roasting pan inside.

Coat the hot pan with the oil and add half of the chopped duck carcasses and necks, turning to coat with the oil. Season with salt. Roast until golden brown, 20 to 30 minutes. Add the onion, celery, and carrot. Roast, stirring occasionally, for 10 minutes, then cook for 15 minutes more. Stir in the tomato paste and roast for 2 minutes. Transfer the mixture to a 4-quart (3.8-L) saucepan. Deglaze the roasting pan with 1 cup (240 ml) water, stirring and scraping up the fond (the browned bits). Pour the water into the saucepan. Add more water to cover the solids by 2 inches (5 cm), at least 12 cups (2.8 L).

Bring to a simmer, then adjust the heat to maintain a slow bubble, uncovered, for 3 hours. Skim the scum that rises to the surface and discard. Press the stock through a fine-mesh sieve. Reserve 7 cups for the rice.

MAKE THE JUS: Preheat the oven to 400°F (205°C) with a roasting pan inside.

Coat the hot pan with the oil and add the remaining chopped duck carcasses and necks, turning to coat with the oil. Season with salt. Roast until golden brown, 20 to 30 minutes. Add the onion, celery, carrot, and garlic. Roast, stirring occasionally, until golden brown. Stir in the tomato paste and roast for 1 minute. Transfer the mixture to a rondeau (wide, shallow pot).

Add just enough duck stock to cover the solids. Bring to a boil, then simmer and reduce the stock until the solids are glazed. Repeat the process three times, adding just enough stock to cover the solids each time after the solids are glazed.

Add enough stock to cover the solids by 1 inch (2.5 cm), bring to a boil, then reduce the heat to maintain a slow simmer. Simmer for 2 hours, then press through a fine-mesh sieve. Transfer to a clean rondeau, bring to a simmer, and reduce until thick enough to coat the back of a spoon.

CONTINUED >>

DUCK RICE

kosher salt and freshly ground white pepper	to taste
duck fat	2 tablespoons
extra-virgin olive oil	¼ cup (60 ml), plus more as needed
Refogado (page 235)	¼ cup (60 ml)
calasparra rice	2 cups (13 ounces/364 g)
chouriço	8 ounces (224 g), casing removed, thinly sliced
pitted Kalamata olives	2 tablespoons, thinly sliced, ¼-inch (6-mm) slices
Duck Skin Cracklins (page 112)	1 recipe
Apricot Puree (page 242)	¼ cup (60 ml), or to taste

MAKE THE RICE: Preheat the oven to 375°F (190°C).

Season the duck breasts with salt and pepper. Place each portion in a sous-vide bag with ½ tablespoon of the duck fat and vacuum seal. Cook for 20 minutes in an immersion circulator set and held at 150°F (65°C). Remove the meat from the bags. You can sear the duck breasts to medum-rare, if you prefer.

Meanwhile, in a heavy 3-quart (2.8-L) rondeau, combine the oil and refogado. Set over medium-low heat and stir in the rice. Continue stirring until the rice is toasted and hot to the touch, about 2 minutes.

Add 6 cups (720 ml) duck stock. Cook, stirring constantly, until the rice has a harder bite than al dente and is still opaque in the center, 8 to 10 minutes. This step is key: Do not let the rice overcook. Transfer to a 14- to 16-inch (35.5- to 40.5-cm) paella pan.

Spread the rice in a flat layer, lightly tapping it with the back of a spoon. Scatter the chouriço, olives, and duck confit on top, then season with salt and pepper. Add 1 cup (240 ml) stock and transfer to the oven.

Bake until the rice is crisped around the edges of the pan and a soccarat crust of rice has formed on the bottom of the pan, about 7 minutes. The liquid should be completely absorbed and the rice an evenly transparent golden hue. Remove from the oven, tent with foil, and let stand for 5 minutes.

Divide the rice among eight serving plates. Slice the duck breasts and arrange on top. Drizzle with the jus. Break the cracklins into pieces and scatter them around the rice. Dollop the apricot puree on the sides of the dishes and serve.

DUCK SKIN CRACKLINS

These are the must-have garnish for the Duck Rice (page 108), but they also make an amazing snack.

SERVES 8

duck skins from 2 whole duck breasts
kosher salt and freshly
ground white pepper to taste

Preheat the oven to 375°F (190°C). Line a half sheet pan with parchment paper.

Carefully scrape off and discard any excess fat from the duck skins. Arrange the duck skins in a single layer on the pan. Season with salt and pepper. Cover with a sheet of parchment paper. Place another half sheet pan on top, and place a cast-iron skillet or other heavy weight on the top pan.

Bake until the skins are golden brown and smell toasty, 10 to 12 minutes. Drain the skins on paper towels. Carefully drain, strain, and reserve the fat for future use. The fat can be refrigerated in an airtight container for up to 1 week.

FARM FRESH

1982 | DANBURY, CONNECTICUT

Farm-to-table may be a popular movement in the restaurant world now—one I champion—but I grew up not knowing any other way of cooking and eating. My parents' families had huge gardens at their homes in Portugal and they kept up that tradition when they arrived in Connecticut. Even when we lived in an apartment building without a proper yard, they planted collard greens, tomatoes, and herbs in the patch of dirt along the driveway. My mom went to the suburban supermarket for cereal, but skipped the fish department for the Portuguese shop that got the freshest catch from the Long Island Sound. (Or she waited until my dad and I went fishing to see what we brought home.)

Since our Portuguese neighbors and relatives did the same, it didn't strike me as particularly remarkable until one spring morning. I knew we were having a big family dinner the next night, but I was surprised to see my aunt Natalia arrive early in the morning. She headed straight to our basement instead of the kitchen, carrying a package I couldn't quite see. My sister and I were watching *The Dukes of Hazard* upstairs when I heard the screeches. Horrible high-pitched squeals from the basement door. As much as I didn't want to look, I did want to see what was happening.

I started down the basement stairs. Once my eyes adjusted to the darkness of the wood-paneled room, I saw my mom and aunt around the corner from the washing machine, perched on turned-over buckets. They each held a sharp, long knife in one hand, a live rabbit in the other. In one quick motion, they'd slit the rabbit's throat, drain the blood, and stack the limp animals in a pile. Each time a rabbit was grabbed by the ears, it would let out that ear-piercing shriek.

Even though a full day passed before we had the rabbit for dinner (they were marinating), I still didn't have much of an appetite. But I had to eat the rabbit rice anyway.

Today, I understand the value of what my mom and aunt did that day. They cooked the way they were raised to cook—by treating the freshest ingredients possible with the utmost respect. They sourced game caught locally and delivered as painless an end as possible by their own hands before cooking it with produce from their gardens. That's what many of us chefs strive for today. It's our responsibility as cooks to create something delicious with focus after taking the life of an animal—or any other living thing.

SPRING CHICKEN RICE

Similar in spirit to the rabbit rice my family makes, this one-pot meal is very creamy and homey. You get a nice bite and sauciness from perfectly cooked rice in this stew. It's a bridge between the seasons with the warming wintery essence of chicken and fresh spring fava beans.

SERVES 4

extra-virgin olive oil	as needed
chicken	1 whole (3 pounds/1.4 kg), cut into 8 pieces
kosher salt and freshly ground white pepper	to taste
Refogado (page 235)	2 tablespoons
fresh bay leaf	1, notches torn every ½ inch (12 mm)
dry white vinho verde	1 cup (240 ml), plus more to taste
Brown Chicken Stock (page 227)	2 quarts (2 L), plus more as needed
bomba or calasparra rice	2 cups (13 ounces/364 g)
fresh thyme	2 sprigs
fresh rosemary	2 sprigs
shucked and shelled fresh fava beans	½ cup (75 g)
fresh parsley leaves	2 tablespoons finely chopped, plus more for garnish

Heat a heavy 8-quart (7.5-L) stockpot over high heat. When hot, add enough oil to generously coat the bottom of the pot. Season the chicken with salt and pepper and add, skin-side down, in a single layer. Don't crowd the pot; work in batches if necessary. Cook until golden brown, about 3 minutes, then flip the pieces and brown the other sides, about 4 minutes more. Transfer to a dish.

Drain the fat from the pan, leaving just a thin layer to coat the bottom. Add 1 tablespoon oil, the refogado, and bay leaf. Cook, stirring and scraping the browned bits from the pan, for 1 minute, then add the vinho verde and chicken thighs and drumsticks. Bring to a boil, then reduce the heat to simmer until the liquid has reduced and is thick, about 3 minutes.

Stir in 2 cups (480 ml) of the stock. Bring to a boil, then reduce the heat to simmer for 15 minutes, turning the chicken pieces occasionally. Season with salt and stir in the rice. Cover and simmer for 5 minutes, then nestle the chicken breast pieces into the mixture and add any accumulated chicken juices and 2 cups (480 ml) more stock. Season to taste with salt.

Bring the stock to a boil, then reduce the heat to maintain a very low simmer and cover. Let the mixture bubble slowly and stir occasionally to prevent the rice from sticking to the bottom and to push any pieces of rice off the chicken. Continue adding stock, 2 cups (480 ml) at a time, so that the rice is covered with liquid the whole time. (If the chicken breasts are cooked through before the rice is tender, transfer them to a dish.) Cook until the rice is al dente and still well-coated in stock, about 25 minutes. The texture should be more like stew than risotto; the rice will also continue to absorb liquid as it sits. Stir in the thyme and rosemary.

Meanwhile, fill a large bowl with ice and water. Bring a large saucepan of water to a boil and salt generously. Add the fava beans and cook, stirring occasionally, until bright green and crisp-tender, about 3 minutes. Immediately transfer to the ice water. When cool, drain well.

Transfer all the chicken pieces to a cutting board and discard the skins and bones. Cut the meat into slices and return to the rice, along with the fava beans and parsley. Season with salt and a splash of vinho verde. Fold gently to mix and season again. Discard the bay leaf, thyme, and rosemary. Garnish with parsley and serve immediately.

QUICK-FIX STOCK

If you don't have the time to make a proper Brown Chicken Stock (page 227), you can simply simmer Chicken Stock (page 226) with cut-up chicken backbones, wings, and neck for about 30 minutes and strain. The flavor won't be nearly as deep, but it'll still be good.

ROAST CHICKEN BREASTS WITH BREAD STUFFING

Historically, the Alentejo region of Portugal was very poor, so their classic dishes reflect the ingenuity home cooks used to make the most of what they had. Migas delivers the flavor of costly meat through the cooking of leftover meat juices with stale bread. The resulting texture is much like American stuffing. I've taken that concept and created my own buttery migas to slide between the skin and flesh of chicken breasts, where it soaks up the cooking juices while basting the meat.

SERVES 2 TO 4

crusty rustic country bread	1 ounce (30 g), cut into 1-inch (2.5-cm) cubes
unsalted butter	½ cup (115 g), softened
fresh lemon thyme leaves	¾ teaspoon
fresh lemon juice	¼ teaspoon
kosher salt and freshly ground white pepper	to taste
chicken	1 whole (3 pounds/1.4 kg)
garlic	1 head, cut in half crosswise
fresh thyme	6 sprigs
fresh rosemary	1 sprig
fresh bay leaf	1, notches torn every ½ inch (12 mm)

Preheat the oven to 375°F (190°C), on the convection setting if you have it.

Place the bread on a baking sheet and toast, stirring occasionally, until very dark golden brown. Let cool completely, then pulse into fine crumbs in a food processor. Pulse in the butter, thyme leaves, and lemon juice. Season with salt and pepper. Transfer to a piping bag fitted with a plain tip.

The key to this dish is the way I butcher the chicken. First, cut out the wishbone by cutting two slits where the bone is at the thick front end, where the breasts meet, and pulling it out. Cut off the chicken legs and wings with the wing tips (keeping the drummettes in place); reserve for another use. Cut off half of the back at the point where the legs meet the back; reserve for another use. You should be left with the whole breast on the rib cage attached to the back with the drumettes on the sides.

Carefully loosen the skin on the breast away from the meat and pipe the butter mixture between the skin and meat. Press the skin to evenly distribute the mixture all over the meat. Pat the chicken skin dry.

Generously season the chicken, inside and out, with salt and pepper. Stuff the cavity with the garlic, thyme sprigs, rosemary, and bay leaf. Tie kitchen twine around the base of the back, across the drumettes, and over the thickest part of the breast to secure the stuffing.

Place the chicken in a large, deep ovenproof skillet and roast for 20 minutes. Baste the bird with the fat in the pan and continue roasting, basting every 5 minutes, until the chicken is cooked through, 20 to 23 minutes more. The thickest part of the breast will feel firm when you press it. Transfer to a serving dish, loosely tent with foil, and let rest for 10 minutes before slicing and serving.

CHICKEN AND ORZO SOUP

Just like the clear, light soup my mom—and moms all over Portugal—makes, this canja is all about pure chicken flavor. I throw in a bit of mint at the end for a distinctive hit of freshness.

SERVES 4

BROTH

chicken	1 whole (3 pounds/1.4 kg)
kosher salt and freshly ground black pepper	to taste
coriander seeds	1 tablespoon
whole black peppercorns	1 teaspoon
fennel seeds	1 teaspoon
fresh bay leaves	2, notches torn every ½ inch (12 mm)
fresh thyme	6 sprigs
fresh parsley	8 sprigs
white onion	1 medium, chopped
carrot	1 medium, peeled and chopped
celery stalk	1 medium, chopped
leek	½ small, chopped
garlic	½ head

MAKE THE BROTH: Cut off the chicken legs, then cut the whole breast into 4 pieces, cutting through the back and bones. Place in a large stockpot and cover with cold water by 1 inch (2.5 cm). Bring to a boil over high heat, then pour out the water along with the scum and foam. This step cleanses the chicken. Wipe any residual scum off the pot.

Cover the chicken with cold water by 1 inch (2.5 cm) again and add a generous pinch of salt. Bring to a boil, then reduce the heat to simmer for 1 hour, skimming and discarding any foam that rises to the surface.

Meanwhile, in a small skillet, heat the coriander, peppercorns, and fennel over medium heat, tossing occasionally, until toasted and fragrant. Transfer to a piece of cheesecloth, along with the bay leaves, thyme, and parsley. Wrap, then tie securely into a sachet. Add to the chicken stock along with the vegetables and a generous pinch of salt. Simmer for 1 hour longer.

CONTINUED >>

CHICKEN SOUP

carrot	1 medium, peeled and diced
celery	1 medium, diced
white onion	1 medium, diced
orzo	½ cup (100 g)
leek	½ small, diced
fresh mint leaves	2 teaspoons, very thinly sliced
fresh dill leaves	2 teaspoons, finely chopped
fresh parsley leaves	1 tablespoon, very finely chopped
fresh lemon juice	to taste
extra-virgin olive oil	to taste

MAKE THE SOUP: Transfer the chicken legs to a plate. You'll add that meat to the soup; the breast meat is too dry and stringy at this point and can be discarded. Strain the soup through a fine-mesh sieve, pressing on the solids.

Return the strained soup to the pot and bring to a boil. Reduce the heat to maintain a steady simmer. Add the carrot and celery and simmer until crisp-tender, about 7 minutes. Add the onion and orzo and simmer until the orzo is al dente, about 10 minutes. While that simmers, discard the skin and bones from the chicken legs and shred or cut the meat into ½-inch (12-mm) chunks. Add to the soup along with the leek and simmer just until the leek is crisp-tender, about 2 minutes.

Stir in the mint, dill, and parsley. Remove from the heat and season with lemon juice and salt. Drizzle with oil and serve immediately.

PARTRIDGE ESCABECHE

Partridge, a nice lean game bird, is traditionally boiled before being lightly pickled. I think that technique kills the flavor, so I cook it sous-vide instead. That also helps trap in the moisture, since the meat doesn't have much fat. If you can't find partridge, try this with quail or even small Cornish game hens.

SERVES 2

SPECIAL EQUIPMENT:
> VACUUM SEALER
> IMMERSION CIRCULATOR

whole black peppercorns	20
whole cloves	10
coriander seeds	1 teaspoon
whole star anise	½
extra-virgin olive oil	as needed
onion	½ large, thinly sliced
garlic cloves	4, very thinly sliced
kosher salt	as needed
Scottish partridges	4 whole (⅓ pound/140 g each)
unsalted butter	4 tablespoons (55 g)
fresh thyme	12 sprigs
fresh bay leaves	2, notches torn every ½ inch (12 mm)
fresh parsley	4 sprigs
Chicken Stock (page 226)	3½ cups (840 ml), cold
sherry vinegar	½ cup (120 ml)
Pickles (page 200)	for serving

In a small skillet, heat the peppercorns, cloves, coriander, and star anise over medium heat, tossing occasionally, until toasted and fragrant. Meanwhile, heat a medium Dutch oven over medium-low heat. Coat the bottom with oil and add the onion, garlic, and a pinch of salt. Sweat, stirring occasionally, until the onion is tender. Stir in the toasted spices and remove from the heat. Let cool to room temperature.

Cut the legs off the partridges and keep the breasts whole. Cut the backs off the breasts and reserve the backs for another use. Heat a large skillet over medium-low heat. Coat the bottom with oil and add 2 tablespoons (30 g) of the butter. Season the partridge breasts with salt and add to the skillet, skin-side down, in a single layer. Cook, turning to evenly brown the skin, until the skin is lightly browned, about 2 minutes. Flip so that the skin-side is up and add 6 thyme sprigs and 1 bay leaf to the skillet. Cook, basting with the fat in the pan, for 2 minutes. Transfer the partridges to a plate and spoon the thyme and bay leaf on top. Repeat with the partridge legs and remaining butter, thyme, and bay leaf. Let cool to room temperature.

In a large bowl, combine the stock, vinegar, and a big pinch of salt. Place the partridge breasts, half of the onion mixture, and half of the stock mixture in a sous-vide bag. Repeat with the partridge legs, remaining onion mixture, and remaining stock mixture. Vacuum seal the bags. Cook for 35 minutes in an immersion circulator set and held at 140°F (60°C).

Open the bags and pour all of the contents into a large bowl. Transfer just the meat to a plate, cover, and refrigerate until cold. Discard the stock and vegetables. Serve the cold meat with the pickles.

GRILLED MARINATED QUAIL

My childhood summers were all about this charred bird served next to cold iceberg salad loaded with cucumbers (page 144). My mom would spatchcock the quail and soak them in paprika-and-onion-spiked wine. I've added more aromatics and a splash of soy for an even richer marinade. If you've never had quail, you have to try it. It's like chicken's sexy, chic cousin—way more savory and juicy, but not as intense as other game. Once it's rested off the grill, just go at it with your hands, gnawing the meat off the bones. There's no other way.

SERVES 4

white onion	½ small, thinly sliced
garlic cloves	3, very thinly sliced
fresh ginger	3-inch (7.5-cm) piece, peeled and very thinly sliced
fresh bay leaves	3, very thinly sliced
fresh thyme	5 sprigs
juniper berries	4, crushed
extra-virgin olive oil	3 tablespoons, plus more for cooking
dry white vinho verde	2 tablespoons
soy sauce	1 tablespoon
pimentón (sweet smoked paprika)	½ teaspoon
crushed red chile flakes	pinch
semi-boneless quail (see below)	4 whole
kosher and Maldon sea salts	to taste

In a container that will hold the quail snugly, mix all of the ingredients aside from the quail and salts. Add the quail and turn to coat well. Cover tightly and refrigerate for at least 2 hours and up to 2 days.

When you're ready to eat, heat a charcoal grill to medium-high. The coals should be ashed over with glowing embers. Wipe the solids off the quail, then coat with more oil and sprinkle both sides with kosher salt. Place on the grill grate, skin-side down, and cook, turning every 2 minutes, until the skin is golden brown and the breasts are medium-rare, about 6 minutes. You want a little char, but don't go crazy.

Transfer to a cutting board and let rest for 5 minutes. Cut off the whole legs, then cut the breasts in halves. Sprinkle with Maldon salt and serve immediately.

HOW TO GET SEMI-BONELESS QUAIL

The easiest way is to buy it that way or to ask your butcher to do it for you, but I actually find deboning very therapeutic. Once you get the hang of it, you will too. Start by getting a pair of kitchen shears and a sharp boning knife. Snip or cut off the neck and wing tips and toss them out. With the knife, cut slits along the wishbone, then pull out the wishbone with your fingers. Flip the bird. With the shears, cut the bird in half lengthwise through the back and splay the bird open, bone-side up. With the knife, gently cut out the backbones and thigh bones. When you get to the breast, cut out the rib cage, then gently run the knife along the central cartilage, being careful to not cut through the skin. Pull the cartilage out with your fingers. The only bones left should be in the wings and drumsticks.

GRILLED MARINATED QUAIL

FOIE GRAS TERRINE WITH CONCORD GRAPE JAM AND CHARRED QUINCE

Every season, I pair my classic French foie gras terrine with fruit, and this fall combination is among my favorites. Quince, a fuzzy, pear-shaped fruit similar in texture and taste to an Asian pear, takes a dip in vanilla syrup, then pickling liquid, for a sharp sweetness that cuts through the richness of the buttery brioche and foie gras.

SERVES 12

SPECIAL EQUIPMENT:
> KITCHEN TORCH

TERRINE

foie gras	1 whole (2 pounds/910 g), lobes separated and deveined
whole milk	as needed
kosher salt	1 tablespoon
pink curing salt	1½ teaspoons
freshly ground white pepper	½ teaspoon

FOIE GRAS WITH QUINCE

sugar	3½ cups (700 g)
vanilla bean	1, split lengthwise, seeds scraped, pod reserved
quince (see Note)	4, peeled, cored, and quartered
All-Purpose Pickling Liquid (page 200)	2 cups (480 ml), plus more as needed
unsalted butter	to taste, softened, for bread
brioche	12 slices
Maldon sea salt	to taste
Concord Grape Jam (page 208)	¼ cup (80 g), or to taste

MAKE THE TERRINE: Place the foie gras in a container that can hold the pieces snugly in a single layer and add enough milk to cover. Cover tightly and refrigerate overnight.

Drain well and pat dry. Wash and dry the container and arrange the foie gras in it again. Sprinkle with the kosher and pink salts and pepper. Cover tightly and refrigerate overnight.

Preheat the oven to 150°F (65°C). Uncover the foie gras, transfer to a half sheet pan and bake until it has rendered some fat and a meat thermometer inserted in the thickest part registers 140°F (60°C).

Line an 8-by-4-inch (20-by-10-cm) loaf pan with plastic wrap, leaving overhang on all four sides. Pack in the foie gras lobes and loose pieces, layer by layer, pressing hard between layers. There should be no gaps or space for air. Cover with the overhang and place a pan of the same size on top. Weigh down the pan with weights or cans and refrigerate for 24 to 48 hours. The longer this cures, the tastier.

MAKE THE FOIE GRAS WITH QUINCE: Combine the sugar, vanilla seeds and pod, and 7 cups (1.7 L) water in a large saucepan. Bring to a boil, stirring to dissolve the sugar. Add the quince, reduce the heat to medium, cover, and simmer until the quince are tender but still holding their shape, about 20 minutes.

With a slotted spoon, transfer the quince to a medium bowl; reserve the simple syrup for another use. Add enough of the pickling liquid to cover the quince. Cover and refrigerate overnight.

When you're ready to serve, remove the quince from the pickling liquid and cut each piece in half lengthwise. Uncover and unwrap the foie gras terrine and cut it into 12 slices. Cut the brioche to match the size of the foie gras slices. Spread butter on one side of each brioche slice. Toast the bread in a broiler, toaster oven, or hot oven until golden brown. Divide among serving plates. Top each toast with a slice of the foie gras terrine and sprinkle with Maldon salt. Arrange the quince slices around the foie gras. Use a kitchen torch to char the quince. Dollop some grape jam on the plates and serve immediately.

NOTE *You can find quince in most farmers' and specialty markets in the fall. Look for unblemished fruit that feels firm. As you peel, core, and cut the fruit, put it into a bowl of cold water with lemon juice to prevent browning.*

FOIE GRAS TERRINE WITH CONCORD GRAPE JAM AND CHARRED QUINCE

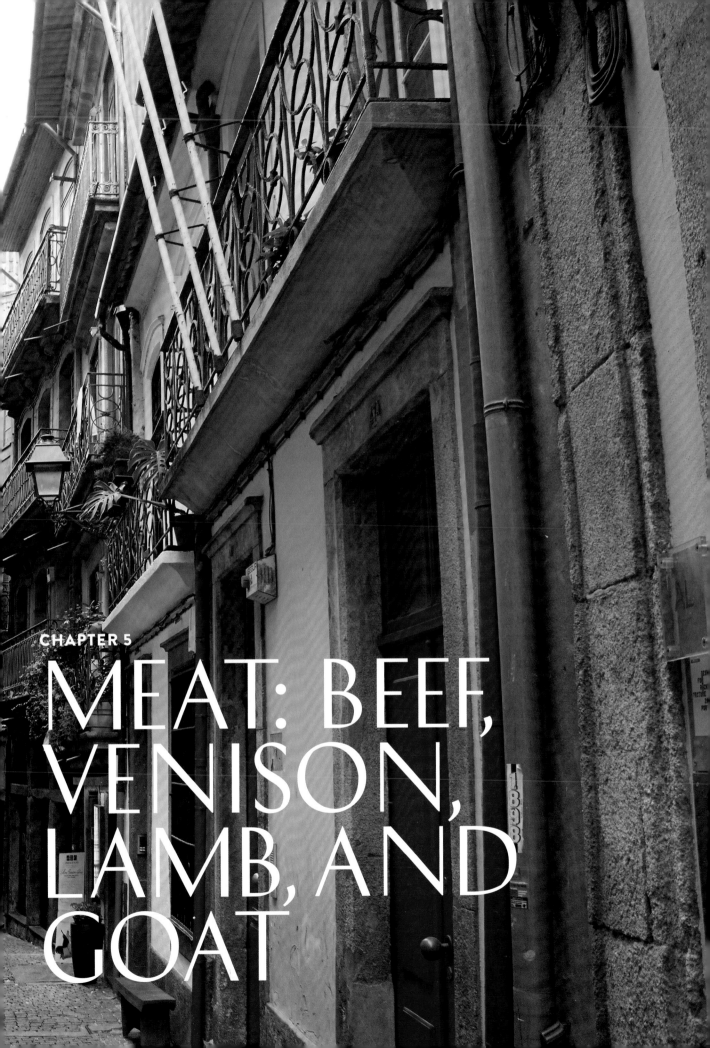

CHAPTER 5

MEAT: BEEF, VENISON, LAMB, AND GOAT

AT THE GRILL AGAIN

2013 | FERREIRÓS DO DÃO

When I pull up to my aunt Alice's house in our family village, Ferreirós do Dão, I'm struck by how the scene is completely unchanged from the last time I was here more than a decade ago. My uncle Anibal stands over the grill, raking the coals. He was doing the exact same thing when I last said good-bye to him. And like that last time, I'm surprising them with my visit. My uncle's eyes crinkle into a smile and he calls out for my aunt. When she sees me through the swinging bead curtain, she runs out of the house and cries, "Oh! George!"

She had first thought I was her son Fernando, who's visiting from Connecticut with his wife, Beth, and two teenage sons. She's waiting for them to return from the store and says she's going to spank his ass if he doesn't get home soon. It's time for lunch.

I'm traveling with Genevieve and my aunt worries that she doesn't have enough food for us and that the food isn't good enough. She's wrong on both counts. But that doesn't stop her from fluttering around us, her children, her grandchildren, and her husband like a nervous butterfly throughout the meal. We sit at their red checker–clothed table in the cool basement and start passing around the tray of steak my uncle has grilled, the huge bowl of salad with greens, tomatoes, and onions from the garden ten feet away, and platters of fries, rice, and bread. Lining the walls of the basement, from the washing machine to the boiler, are jugs of homemade wine and my cousin pours us generous glasses.

My aunt circles us with the platters, smiling and pressing, "More? More?" My cousins, at the end of their two-week stay with their grandparents, say, "It's incredible, right? This is how we eat lunch here every day." Like me, they were born and raised in Connecticut. I can see how they're reconnecting with their roots through this typical lunch of charred thin fillets and fresh garden salad. Being back at my aunt's table, I'm hit with such powerful memories of my time with my family—both in this village and in Connecticut. I've always felt connected to my cultural identity, especially when I've finished a homey meal and am sipping the jeropiga liqueur my uncle brewed and eating the rich sponge cake my aunt baked.

When I return to my aunt's house two days later to say good-bye, I start laughing. Uncle Anibal is there again, at the grill, lighting the coals for another round of steak. I plan to return well before another ten years go by, but when I do, I fully expect to see Uncle Anibal in the same spot where I left him.

BRAISED OXTAIL

coriander seeds	1½ teaspoons
black peppercorns	1 teaspoon
cumin seeds	1 teaspoon
mustard seeds	1 teaspoon
cinnamon stick	¼
espelette pepper (see Note)	½ teaspoon
dry red wine	1 cup (240 ml)
red wine vinegar	½ cup (120 ml)
canola oil	as needed
oxtails	2½ pounds (1.2 kg), each 2 inches (5 cm) thick
kosher salt and freshly ground white pepper	to taste
white onion	1 large, diced
carrot	1 medium, peeled and diced
celery stalks	2 medium, diced
garlic cloves	6, chopped
fresh bay leaf	1, notches torn every ½ inch (12 mm)
tomato paste	1½ tablespoons

Toasted spices infuse the meat with their aromas during the long braise and shine through in the reduced sauce.

SERVES 4

Preheat the oven to 300°F (150°C).

In a small skillet, heat the coriander, peppercorns, cumin, mustard seeds, and cinnamon over medium heat, tossing occasionally, until toasted and fragrant. Let cool completely, then transfer to a spice grinder and add the espelette pepper. Pulse until finely ground. Transfer to a small bowl and stir in the wine and vinegar.

Heat a large cast-iron cocotte or Dutch oven over high heat until it is very hot. Lightly coat with oil and heat until almost smoking. Generously season both sides of the oxtails with salt and pepper and cook until charred, about 2 minutes, then flip and char the other sides, about 2 minutes longer. Transfer to a plate.

Add the onion, carrot, celery, garlic, bay leaf, and a pinch of salt to the cocotte. Reduce the heat to medium and cook, stirring occasionally, until lightly browned. Add the spice mixture and cook, stirring and scraping the browned bits occasionally, until almost all of the liquid has evaporated. Add the tomato paste and cook, stirring, for 2 minutes.

Return the oxtails and the accumulated juices to the cocotte and add enough water to cover by 1 inch (2.5 cm). Bring to a simmer, cover, and transfer to the oven. Braise until the meat is tender, about 5 hours.

Transfer the oxtails to a serving dish; you can serve them on the bone or pick the meat into serving pieces and discard the bones. Strain the cooking liquid through a fine-mesh sieve into a medium saucepan, pressing on the solids to extract as much liquid as possible. Bring to a boil and cook until reduced to a glaze. Spoon over the oxtails and serve.

NOTE *Espelette pepper, often labeled piment d'espelette, is ground from dried espelette peppers cultivated and grown in the southwestern Basque region of France. It's available in specialty markets and online.*

GLAZED LAMB SHOULDER

Cooking the tough lamb shoulder sous-vide tenderizes the meat while keeping it moist. To heighten the rich lamb flavor, I cook the meat in a concentrated lamb stock.

SERVES 4

SPECIAL EQUIPMENT:
> VACUUM SEALER
> IMMERSION CIRCULATOR

kosher salt	½ cup (125 g)
lamb shoulder	1 whole, tough tissues removed
Garlic Oil (page 241)	1½ cups (360 ml)
Lamb Jus (page 230)	1 cup (240 ml)
fresh thyme	1 bunch

In a large bowl, dissolve the salt in 3 quarts (2.8 L) water. Add the lamb shoulder, cover tightly, and refrigerate for 24 hours.

Remove the lamb from the brine and pat dry with paper towels. Place the shoulder and the remaining ingredients in a large sous-vide bag and vacuum seal. Cook for 36 hours in an immersion circulator set and held at 145°F (62°C).

Let the meat rest in the bag for 10 minutes, then transfer the bag to a large bowl of ice and water. Remove the meat from the bag; discard the cooking liquid. Serve the lamb whole or in pieces.

VENISON IN JUNIPER-PEPPER CRUST

Venison may be lean, but its dense flesh has a deep, meaty flavor. To prevent the tenderloin from drying out, I wrap it in dough before roasting it. The blast of heat from the oven infuses the meat with the savory spices from the crust.

SERVES 4

juniper berries	1½ teaspoons
coriander seeds	1 teaspoon
whole black peppercorns	1 teaspoon
all-purpose flour	2 cups (250 g), plus more for kneading and rolling
kosher salt	to taste
egg whites	2 large
extra-virgin olive oil	as needed
venison tenderloins	2 whole (8 ounces/225 g each)
Sweet Carrot Custards (page 179)	1 recipe

Preheat the oven to 400°F (205°C). Line a half sheet pan with parchment paper.

In a small skillet, heat the juniper, coriander, and peppercorns over medium heat, tossing occasionally, until toasted. Let cool completely, then pulse in a spice grinder until coarsely ground.

In the bowl of a stand mixer fitted with the paddle attachment, beat the flour, spices, and salt to taste on low speed until well mixed. Beat in the egg whites until well combined, then beat in ⅔ cup (165 ml) cold water until a dough forms. Transfer to a lightly floured work surface and knead until smooth. Cover and refrigerate for 15 minutes.

Cut each venison tenderloin in half crosswise. Heat a large skillet over medium heat and coat with oil. Add the venison and cook until lightly colored on all sides. Let rest for 5 minutes. Tie each piece with kitchen twine at 1-inch (2.5-cm) intervals.

Cut the dough into four even pieces. On a lightly floured surface, with a lightly floured rolling pin, roll one piece of dough into a rectangle ¼ inch (6 mm) thick, 3 inches (7.5 cm) wider than the length of one piece of tenderloin, and 1 inch (2.5 cm) longer than the diameter of the tenderloin. Repeat with the remaining dough. Place one piece of tenderloin in one dough rectangle and wrap the dough around it, pressing the ends to seal. Fold in the sides and press the dough to completely encase and seal the venison. Repeat with the remaining dough and venison.

Place the wrapped venison on the prepared sheet pan, seam-sides down. Bake until the crusts are golden, about 5 minutes. Let rest on the pan for 3 minutes, then transfer to serving plates, along with the carrot custards. To eat, discard the dough and kitchen twine and cut the venison.

BABY GOAT WITH BEETS, CINNAMON-CLOVE YOGURT, AND CHARRED BREAD EMULSION

I love this dish. It's based on the simplest ingredient—day-old bread, which my mom and family in Portugal taught me to always use. That and underappreciated meats like baby goat. Here, I've turned the bread into a luxurious truffle-like emulsion and the goat into a melt-in-your-mouth confit.

SERVES 10

YOGURT

canola oil	¼ cup (60 ml)
whole star anise	3
cinnamon sticks	2
whole cloves	2
cardamom pods	2
agar agar	½ teaspoon
goat's-milk yogurt	1 cup (240 ml)

MAKE THE YOGURT: In a small saucepan, heat the oil to 175°F (80°C). Add the star anise, cinnamon, cloves, and cardamom. Let steep for 1 hour. Strain out the spices, reserving the oil.

Meanwhile, in a small saucepan, combine the agar agar with ¼ cup (60 ml) of the yogurt. Heat to a simmer, stirring. Transfer to a blender, along with the remaining ¾ cup (180 ml) yogurt and blend well. Pour into a 1-inch- (2.5-cm-) deep pan and refrigerate until the mixture sets into a hard gel. Cut up the gel and scoop it from the pan into a blender. Puree until very smooth. With the machine running, add the spice oil in a steady stream. Blend until emulsified.

CONTINUED >>

CHARRED BREAD EMULSION

day-old bread	3 (1-inch-/2.5-cm-thick) slices
extra-virgin olive oil	as needed
Coriander Dashi (page 231)	1½ cups (360 ml), hot
crème fraîche	3 cups (720 ml), at room temperature
orange	1
soy sauce	to taste

Baby Goat Terrine (page 139)	1 recipe
extra-virgin olive oil	as needed
Smoked Baby Beets (page 178)	1 recipe

MAKE THE CHARRED BREAD EMULSION: Preheat the oven to 375°F (190°C). Prepare a grill by heating a mixture of all-natural briquettes and hardwood lump charcoal until hot.

Drizzle the bread with olive oil. Grill until the bread is charred and grill marks appear, turning occasionally. Transfer to a sheet pan and bake until as dry as a crouton. When cool enough to handle, break the bread into small pieces and transfer to a blender. Pour the dashi over and puree until very smooth. Press through a medium-mesh sieve into a large bowl. Whisk in the crème fraîche. Zest some of the orange into the mixture to taste and season with soy sauce.

Cut the goat terrine into ten even blocks. Heat a large skillet over medium-low heat. Coat with olive oil and add a few of the blocks. Cook on one side until very lightly browned. Transfer to a sheet pan. Repeat with the remaining blocks. Transfer to the oven and bake until heated through, about 5 minutes.

Arrange the goat terrine, bread emulsion, yogurt, and beets on serving plates.

BABY GOAT TERRINE

Occasionally, I'll dress this up with sauces like the Charred Bread Emulsion (opposite), but it's also fantastic on its own with Pickles (page 200) and good mustard.

SERVES 10

baby goat	1 whole (25 pounds/11.3 kg)
extra-virgin olive oil	2 cups, plus more as needed
dry white vinho verde	1 cup (240 ml)
white onion	1, thinly sliced
garlic cloves	6, crushed
fresh bay leaves	6, notches torn every ½ inch (12 mm)
pimentón (sweet smoked paprika)	2 tablespoons
kosher salt and	
freshly ground white pepper	to taste
duck fat	2 quarts (2 L) or as needed, melted
Activa transglutaminase (see Note)	as needed

First, butcher the goat: Cut off its two shoulders, two legs, then split the ribs into two portions. You can also ask your butcher to do this for you or buy those pieces individually. In a pan that holds the goat snugly, combine the oil, vinho verde, onion, garlic, bay leaves, and pimentón. Add the cut-up goat and turn to coat well. Cover tightly and refrigerate overnight.

Preheat the oven to 200°F (90°C).

Remove the goat from the marinade, wiping off any excess. Discard the marinade. Generously season all the pieces with salt and pepper. Divide the pieces between two roasting pans (one leg, one shoulder, one rib portion in each) that hold them in a single layer. Divide the duck fat between the pans. The fat should come one-third of the way up the goat. Cover the pans tightly with foil. Transfer to the oven and cook for 10 hours.

Uncover the pans. When the goat is cool enough to handle, pull the meat in large pieces from the bones; discard the bones. Cut the meat into 2-by-1-inch (5-by-2.5-cm) pieces.

Line a half sheet pan with plastic wrap. Place half of the goat pieces in the pan in a single layer without gaps. Press the meat to form a flat, even layer. Lightly dust the meat with the transglutaminase. Top with the other half of the goat, pressing the meat to form a flat, even layer. Cover tightly with plastic wrap, place another half sheet pan on top, and place a cast-iron skillet or other heavy weight on the top pan. Refrigerate at least overnight or for up to 2 days.

When you're ready to serve, cut the terrine into slices.

NOTE *Activa transglutaminase, known as "meat glue" among chefs, helps bind this terrine together. It's available in professional kitchen supply stores.*

PORTUGUESE WINES

It wasn't until I visited Herdade do Esporão, a sustainable winery in the heart of the Alentejo region, that I realized the extent of the country's wine production. As I drove along the roads through their vineyards—careful to avoid hitting any hares protected as part of their nature preserve—all I could see to the horizon were vines. And this winery is one of the country's smaller, albeit higher-quality, producers in only one of many wine-growing regions. What I love about Portuguese wines is that they're affordable and perfect for pairing with food and for cooking. Here, then, is a brief introduction to the wide world of Portuguese wines:

If we have a national varietal, vinho verde is it. The name means "green wine," and many take that to indicate that it's meant to be drunk young, which it is. (It may also refer to the verdant coastal valleys of the Minho region, where this wine is made.) Even though the white variety dominates, there are also great red and rosé vinho verdes.

I love a good, dry white vinho verde with a balance of fresh minerality and acidity, a hint of citrus, and a slight effervescence. It's the wine I grew up smelling in my mom's marinades and the wine I use most now when I cook. Look for the latest vintage, chill it, and enjoy. It pairs perfectly with seafood, complementing clean preparations like just-shucked oysters and cutting through the richness of something as meaty as octopus.

A dry vinho verde rosé has an even crisper acidity and lighter body, making it ideal as an aperitif. Even though red vinho verdes are a deep, dark red color, they tend to taste light and tangy, with a hint of fruit. In Portugal, they're often poured with grilled sardines or charcuterie.

Beyond vinho verde, there are countless options from hundreds of both native and international grape varieties in Portugal. It's easiest to choose what you like by the region in which it grows. Full-bodied whites with richer, softer textures come from the hot, sunny Alentejo in the south. Intense whites with high minerality and a full body hail from the Douro and Trás-os-Montes in the northeast. These are sometimes fermented or matured in oak barrels, and the reserve whites tend to be the most full-bodied. These whites are great with richer seafood dishes and work well with smoky flavors.

For elegant yet intense well-balanced reds, look to the Dão region. They maintain a good acidity and often have aromatic hints of fruit. This makes them versatile enough to serve with poultry or red meat.

The Alentejo is also home to rich, round, full-bodied reds with lots of fruit. As with the whites, some spend time in oak and end up even denser. You can find similar wines from the Tejo. The nice thing about these wines is that they're low in tannins, which makes them ideal for pairing with food. I enjoy them with all kinds of meat, from game to offal to charcuterie.

For more robust reds, the northern Douro Valley and neighboring Trás-os-Montes produce a range of flavors, from rich fruit to acidic and herbaceous. They're fairly tannic early on. Once they mature, the tannins mellow, making these wines versatile and delicious with both meat and seafood stews. The Bairrada region also produces robust reds, somewhat softer and more savory than those of the north.

Over the past decade, Portuguese wine imports to the United States have tripled, and I know that they are just going to keep rising. I'll drink to that.

The vineyard and winery of Herdade do Esporão produce delicious wines.

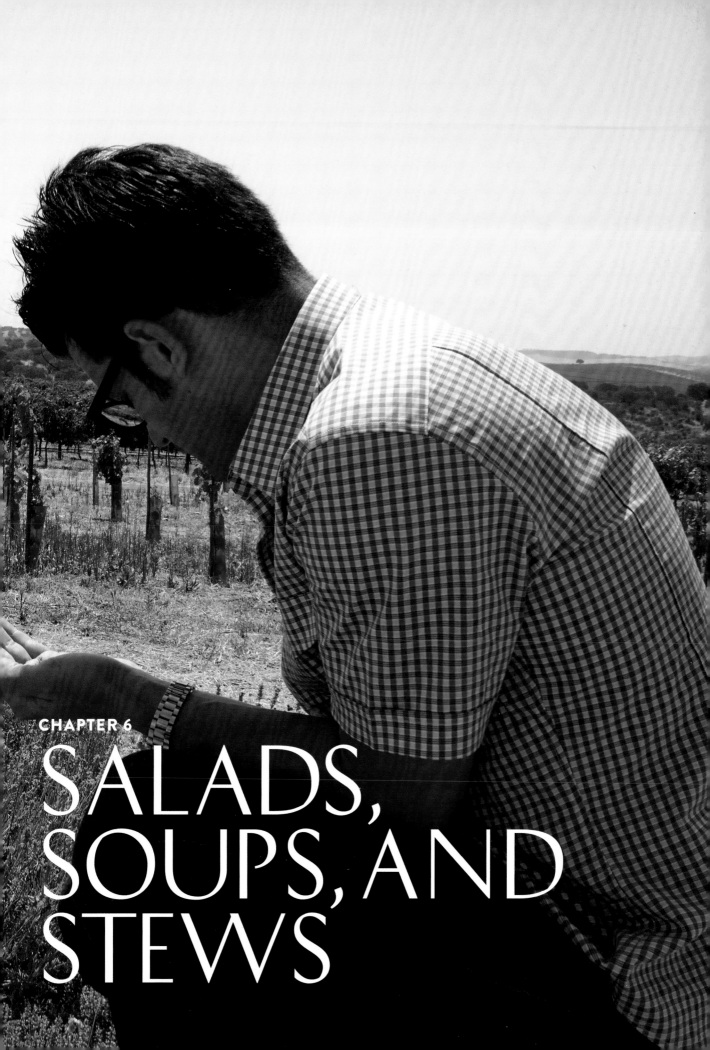

CHAPTER 6
SALADS, SOUPS, AND STEWS

ICEBERG, CUCUMBER, AND TOMATO SALAD

Every summer, my mom picked ripe, warm tomatoes from our garden, then walked down the street to her sister's house to pluck a cucumber and an onion. When she got home, she'd throw together this salad and serve it with everything from Marinated Grilled Pork Tenderloin (page 86) to Tomato Rice (page 188). I love the simplicity of this. Iceberg gets looked down on, but when it's fresh and crunchy, it's so good.

SERVES 8

iceberg lettuce	1 small head, leaves torn
white onion	1 medium, halved and very thinly sliced
cucumber	1 medium, peeled, halved, and thinly sliced
tomatoes	2 large ripe, cored, halved, and cut into ¼-inch (6-mm) slices
fresh parsley leaves	3 tablespoons
red wine vinegar	¼ cup (60 ml)
extra-virgin olive oil	6 tablespoons (90 ml)
kosher salt and freshly ground white pepper	to taste

In a large salad bowl, combine the lettuce, onion, cucumber, tomatoes, and parsley. When you're ready to serve, whisk together the vinegar, oil, and a pinch each of salt and pepper in a small bowl. Pour over the salad and very, very gently toss with your hands. You don't want the tomatoes to break.

Dig in right away! This gets soggy fast, so you've got to eat it quickly.

A TALE OF TWO VILAS

My first night in the southern coastal region of the Algarve, I dine at the two-Michelin-starred restaurant of the phenomenal Vila Joya Hotel in Albufeira. Chef Dieter Koschina produces a perfectly executed tasting menu and his sommelier matches it to beautiful wines. The "dining room" on the stone patio overlooking their private beach has the kind of seaside view you see only in postcards. I can't imagine a more picturesque meal. But the next night, I get to experience one. It's nothing like the haute cuisine refinement of Vila Joya; it's another vila, another style of tasting menu, and just as beautiful.

Even though I get hints of Portuguese seasonings in Dieter's dishes, I find a taste of true Algarve cuisine at Vila Lisa. I check out of the quiet elegance of the Vila Joya and into the chic Bela Vista Hotel in the Miami-like city of Portimao. After a rough start with my phone's navigation system, I make it out of the beach-side Portimao into the impossible-to-pronounce village of Mexilhoeira Grande in the seaside hills above. With yellow-shuttered windows glowing in the dark, quiet village, Restaurant Vila Lisa occupies a white-washed, blue-trimmed farmhouse, furnished only with communal picnic tables. Along one wall are pyramids of wine bottles, on the others are Miró-esque paintings, created by the chef.

As soon as I sit down, the sandal-clad server sets down a basket of locally baked crusty bread and a plate of mild fresh goat cheese and fat-laced hunks of morcella sausage. She twists the cap off the kind of huge plastic jug I've seen used for car oil and pours a carafe of their homemade white wine. A second later, she sets down cold plates of smashed potatoes and garlic and a salad of tomatoes and onions laced with house-cured tuna, both bathed in a fruity olive oil and flecked with dried oregano. I'm blown away by how good it is.

Everything that follows makes me feel like I'm at home. A brothy rice soup is studded with thimble-size sweet clams, octopus comes glistening with potatoes and peppers, a whole pork shank slides right off the bone in juicy hunks. And for the first time on my trip, I swear my mom's the one in the kitchen. A stew of creamy brick-red beans, shreds of braised meat, and soft macaroni noodles tastes exactly like the one my mom cooked for me when I was a kid. It's the ultimate comfort food. So is the dessert: dried-fig-and-almond balls made with the fragrant fruits and nuts from the surrounding hillsides.

Long after I down their local after-dinner licorice liqueur, I keep thinking about the potato and tuna salads. They were so simple and so damn satisfying. I can count the number of ingredients on one hand. It's the spirit of Algarve cuisine to take fresh, local ingredients, cook them perfectly or not at all, and season them with intense olive oil, sea salt, and oregano. It's also a reminder of what I need to do as a chef. It's easy to get wrapped up in trying to figure out what the undercover Michelin guide critics expect, how to choreograph the picture-perfect meal, which events to sign up for. But what I want—need—to remember is that the heart of what I do is what I experienced at Vila Lisa. It's to feed people dishes that remind them how tasty something as humble as a boiled potato with olive oil, sea salt, and wild oregano can be. It's to make food so satisfying and soulful that anyone eating it will feel completely at home.

TUNA, TOMATO, AND ONION SALAD

Sometimes, the simplest things in life are best. When I sat down to this salad at a homey restaurant in Portugal's Algarve region, I was hit by the pure flavors accented by wild oregano. Buying great tuna is key to this dish; I like Cuca Bonita Del Norte en Aceite de Oliva.

SERVES 4

heirloom tomatoes	2 pounds (910 g), a mix of sizes and colors
white onion	1 medium, very thinly sliced
tuna packed in olive oil	2 (4-ounce/112-g) cans
fresh oregano blossoms and leaves	2 tablespoons
fresh lemon thyme leaves	2 teaspoons
extra-virgin olive oil	to taste
sherry and/or date vinegar	to taste
Maldon sea salt	to taste
freshly ground white pepper	to taste

Core the tomatoes and cut into slices and wedges. Arrange on a serving plate with the onion. Break the tuna into chunks and scatter over the vegetables, along with its oil. Top with the oregano and thyme, drizzle with oil and vinegar, and season with salt and pepper.

SARDINES WITH SPRING GREENS AND ALMONDS

Fresh sardines can be found all over Portugal and, thankfully, increasingly here. I love them in this simple salad with sweet vinegar, peppery greens, and buttery almonds.

SERVES 4

unsalted butter	½ tablespoon
extra-virgin olive oil	as needed
whole blanched almonds	3 tablespoons
kosher salt and freshly ground white pepper	to taste
fresh sardines	8, filleted, bones removed
Wondra flour	as needed
lemon wedges	to taste
fleur de sel	to taste
date or raspberry vinegar	1 tablespoon
shallot	1 tablespoon very thinly sliced
spring greens, such as arugula, cress, purslane, pea shoots, or edible flowers, preferably a combination	4 cups (115 g) packed, tough stems removed
Tomato Confit (page 243; optional)	for serving

In a small skillet, heat the butter and 1 teaspoon oil over medium heat. Add the almonds and cook, stirring, until golden brown, about 1 minute. Drain on paper towels, then sprinkle with kosher salt.

Pat the sardines very dry, then sprinkle with salt and pepper. Lightly dust with flour. Heat a large skillet over high heat until very hot. Lightly coat the bottom with oil and heat until almost smoking. Add the sardines in a single layer. Cook, lightly pressing the sardines flat with a spatula as they curl, just until golden brown, about 1 minute, and then flip quickly. Cook for 5 seconds more and immediately transfer to a plate. You don't want them to overcook; only the edges of the fillets should be white. Squeeze lemon juice over the sardines and sprinkle with fleur de sel.

In a large bowl, whisk the vinegar with 2 tablespoons oil. Season with salt and pepper. Add the shallot, greens, and a pinch each of salt and pepper and toss to coat. Divide among serving plates along with the sardines, almonds, and tomato confit, if using.

HEIRLOOM TOMATO SALAD WITH BLACK OLIVES AND HERBS

Basil's a must for ripe summer tomatoes, but mint also brings out their complex sweetness. So does a high-quality fruity olive oil.

SERVES 4

heirloom tomatoes	2½ pounds (1.2 kg), a mix of colors, cored and cut into ½-inch (12-mm) slices
pitted Kalamata olives	14, halved lengthwise
extra-virgin olive oil	to taste
fig or balsamic vinegar	to taste
fresh mint leaves	1 tablespoon
fresh basil leaves	½ tablespoon
Maldon sea salt or fleur de sel	to taste
freshly ground white pepper	to taste

Arrange the tomatoes and olives on a serving platter. Generously drizzle oil over the tomatoes until they're shiny and well coated. Add about half the amount of vinegar by dropping it on top to color the plate a bit. I use a little eye dropper bottle, but you can just put your thumb against the vinegar bottle's opening to add the vinegar by drops.

Scatter the mint and basil on top, then season with salt and pepper.

COUNTRY COOKING

The wine bar and restaurant at the Herdade do Esporão are as sleek as any in New York City. But that's not where we're eating tonight. Antonio Roquette, Esporão's head of tourism, and Miguel Vaz Oliveira, the restaurant's chef, want to take me and Genevieve to what they call "an authentic local place for real Alentejo cuisine." And that's exactly what O Chico is. Chico's the nickname of Chef Francisco, who's been behind the stove at this taberna for more than twenty-five years. With his wire-rimmed glasses and gap-toothed smile, he's like a jolly, round grandpa always ready with another story. And he is. He's perfected the hearty, rustic dishes of this landlocked region and he gives me a taste of nearly everything he's got, along with a running narrative of what we're eating.

That includes queijo de ovelha, a funky sheep's-milk cheese made nearby, and paiola, a regional sausage made with pork liver and seasoned with garlic and coriander. Fried horse-mackerel comes with onions escabeche, little pies are stuffed with chicken, whole eggs are simmered in chunky tomatoes, and peppers are roasted until they collapse. And that's just the first round. From there, the dishes get even richer. Migas, made by soaking bread crumbs in meat juices, come in a pork and a cauliflower version, both served with hunks of fried pork. Meaty mushrooms are scrambled with eggs, local melon-patch beans are cooked with whole quail eggs, and pig's trotters have been stewed with coriander. The most surprising dish is a combination of favas and morcella sausage. The favas hover somewhere between fresh and dried and when I ask Chef Francisco about it, he explains:

"Ah, the favas. I dry them with the skins on, then soak them and simmer them whole until they're soft enough to eat. Listen, I'll tell you everything, give you any recipe you want. The one thing I can't give you? My palate." (I now feel all I'm fit for is sweeping the kitchen floor.)

He smiles with the assurance of a chef who's been running his own place for decades and heads back to the kitchen to bring out our main courses. In the Alentejo, soup is the entrée, not the starter. But stew may be a better word for it. We start with a cardoons soup in which soft goat cheese is melted into the broth, then move on to a purslane soup studded with whole garlic cloves. To finish, we have dogfish soup, a staple in the Alentejo. Like a small shark, dogfish is meaty and its silky fillets flake into the creamy broth. I'm as full as I've ever been, but it's been an eye-opening introduction to the country cuisine of the farms and fields and I'm ready for more.

COLLARD GREENS SOUP

CALDO VERDE

The national dish of Portugal is this humble potato, sausage, and greens soup. Growing up, I polished off bowls at my aunt Natalia's place every Christmas and at the Portuguese-American Club all year long. It defines the culture and the people: warm, soulful, and easy to love.

SERVES 4

extra-virgin olive oil	as needed
cured chouriço	1 (5-inch/12-cm) piece
white onion	½ small, thinly sliced
garlic cloves	4, thinly sliced
kosher salt	as needed
Yukon gold potatoes	4 large (1 pound 10 ounces/735 g), peeled and cut into 1-inch (2.5-cm) chunks
collard greens	1 pound (455 g)

Heat a large saucepot over medium-low heat. Coat the bottom with oil, then add the chouriço, onion, garlic, and a pinch of salt. Cook, stirring occasionally, until the onion is tender but not browned, about 10 minutes.

Add the potatoes and enough water to cover them by 1 inch (2.5 cm). Raise the heat to bring the water to a boil, then reduce the heat to simmer for 30 minutes.

Transfer the chouriço to a cutting board. When cool enough to handle, cut into ⅛-inch- (3-mm-) thick slices. Meanwhile, continue simmering the potatoes, replenishing the water as needed to keep it 1 inch (2.5 cm) above the potatoes, until they're very, very soft, about 45 minutes longer.

While the potatoes cook, prepare the collards. In Portugal, this is called the "caldo verde cut." Strip the leaves off the tough stems and ribs, then stack a few leaves and roll them very tightly into a cylinder. Cut the cylinder crosswise into very, very thin strips (1/16 to ⅛ inch/2 to 3 mm), then cut those strips into 1-inch (2.5-cm) lengths. Repeat with the remaining collards.

Fill a large bowl with ice and water. Bring a large saucepan of water to a boil and salt it generously. Add the collards and cook, stirring vigorously, until bright green and crisp-tender, about 2 minutes. Immediately transfer to the ice water. When cool, drain well.

Using a blender, puree the potatoes with their cooking liquid until very smooth. While pureeing, drizzle in 2 tablespoons oil. Press the mixture through a fine-mesh sieve into a large saucepan. Stir in more water to create a soupy consistency. Bring to a simmer, then fold in the onion mixture, collards, and chouriço. Season with salt. Divide among serving bowls and drizzle with oil.

TOMATO, BREAD, AND EGG STEW

AÇORDA

At its core, açorda, an Alentejo specialty, is bread soaked in broth. It's soupier than migas is usually and can also include tomatoes and be thickened with eggs. I keep my version lighter, with fresh lime zest and cilantro, but I still get a warming richness from the thick soup.

SERVES 4

whole-wheat country bread	3½ cups (98 g) of 1-inch (2.5-cm) cubes (from ½ large loaf)
extra-virgin olive oil	3 tablespoons, plus more as needed
white onion	1 small, finely diced
garlic cloves	3, minced
kosher salt and freshly ground white pepper	to taste
fresh bay leaf	1, notches torn every ½ inch (12 mm)
tomato paste	1 teaspoon
heirloom or beefsteak tomatoes	3 medium, peeled, seeded, and diced (1½ cups/280 g)
coriander seeds	1½ teaspoons, toasted and ground
pimentón (smoked sweet paprika)	1 teaspoon, plus more to taste
crushed red chile flakes	pinch
Vegetable Stock (page 226)	2 cups (480 ml)
fresh cilantro leaves	½ cup (15 g), finely chopped
eggs	2 large, beaten
freshly grated lime zest	¼ teaspoon
Maldon sea salt	to taste

Preheat the oven to 300°F (150°C). Spread the bread in a single layer on a half sheet pan and bake until toasted, dry, and crunchy. Let cool completely.

Heat 2 tablespoons of the oil in a medium cast-iron casserole over medium heat. Add the onion, garlic, and a big pinch of kosher salt. Stir in the bay leaf. Cook, stirring occasionally, until the onions are just translucent, about 7 minutes.

Add the tomato paste and another tablespoon of oil and cook, stirring occasionally, for 3 minutes. Add the tomatoes, coriander, pimentón, chile flakes, and a big pinch of kosher salt. Stir well, bring to a simmer, and simmer until the mixture is thick and the flavors are really concentrated, about 10 minutes.

Gently fold in the bread and let it soak up the juices. Drizzle with oil. Add 1 cup (240 ml) of the stock and fold in gently. You don't want the bread to shred. Continue adding the stock, ½ cup (120 ml) at a time, folding gently after each addition. The mixture will be wet and the bread will break down a little, but you want the cubes to hold their shape. The more you work it now, the gummier the mixture will become. Discard the bay leaf.

Gently fold in the cilantro and eggs until the eggs are heated through. You don't want to actually scramble the eggs, you just want them to enrich the mixture. Drizzle with oil and garnish with lime zest, more pimentón, and Maldon salt. Serve immediately.

CABBAGE AND TOMATO SOUP

My mom makes this soup chunky and sometimes even adds noodles. I've kept the rustic texture, but also added an underlying smoothness by pureeing half the soup first.

SERVES 8

green cabbage	1 large head (2¾ pounds/1.3 kg)
extra-virgin olive oil	as needed
white onion	1 medium, quartered and thinly sliced
garlic cloves	6, thinly sliced
fresh bay leaves	2, notches torn every ½ inch (12 mm)
kosher salt	to taste
tomatoes	2 medium
Vegetable Stock (page 226)	1 quart (960 ml), plus more as needed
pimentón (smoked sweet paprika)	1 tablespoon plus 1 teaspoon

Remove 8 large outer green leaves from the cabbage and cut out and discard the ribs. Cut the leaves into 1½-inch (4-cm) squares. Reserve. Cut out the core and thick white ribs from the remaining cabbage and discard. Thinly slice the remaining leaves and reserve separately.

Heat a 12-quart (11.3-L) saucepot over medium-low heat. Coat the bottom with oil, then add the onion, garlic, and bay leaves. Season with salt and sweat, stirring occasionally, until the onion is tender, about 10 minutes.

Meanwhile, fill a large bowl with ice and water. Bring a large saucepan of water to a boil. Slit an "x" in the base of each tomato and drop in the boiling water. Let sit for 10 seconds, then transfer to the ice water. Take the tomatoes out of the ice water, then peel, cut in quarters, and discard the seeds. Transfer the flesh to a blender and puree until smooth. Add to the onion mixture, bring to a simmer, and cook until reduced and thick, about 5 minutes.

While the tomatoes simmer, bring the saucepan of water back to a boil and salt generously. Add the outer cabbage leaves and cook until bright green and crisp-tender, about 4 minutes. Immediately transfer to the ice water. When cool, drain well.

To the tomato mixture, stir in the stock and ½ teaspoon of the pimentón. Bring to a boil, then reduce the heat to simmer for 15 minutes. Discard the bay leaves. Add the remaining sliced cabbage, 1 tablespoon oil, another ½ teaspoon pimentón, and a generous pinch of salt. Bring to a boil, then reduce the heat to simmer until the cabbage is tender, about 35 minutes.

Using a blender, puree until very smooth. Blend in the remaining 1 tablespoon pimentón and return the soup to a simmer. Fold in the outer green cabbage leaves. Season with salt and drizzle with oil. Serve immediately.

ROASTED
SQUASH SOUP

Super silky and buttery, this is my ideal fall soup. The spices are subtle, but they come through in the sweet squash. You can garnish this with toasted nuts if you like crunch, Concord grapes if you prefer sweet, or seared bay scallops for a complete meal.

SERVES 4

unsalted butter	¼ cup (55 g)
cinnamon sticks	2
juniper berries	15
whole star anise	1
green cardamom pods	4
coriander seeds	2 teaspoons
butternut squash	1 medium (2 pounds/910 g), trimmed, quartered lengthwise, and seeded
sugar pumpkin	1 small (1½ pounds/680 g), trimmed, quartered, and seeded
kosher salt and freshly ground white pepper	to taste
Vegetable Stock (page 226)	1½ cups (360 ml), hot, plus more as needed
extra-virgin olive oil	to taste

Preheat the oven to 375°F (190°C).

In a small saucepan, combine the butter, cinnamon, juniper, star anise, cardamom, and coriander. Cook over medium-low heat, stirring, until the butter is light golden brown and the spices are fragrant, about 6 minutes.

Arrange the squash and pumpkin, cut-sides up, in a single layer in a large roasting pan. Generously season with salt, then drizzle with the butter and spices. Cover the pan with foil and bake until a knife slides easily through the squash and pumpkin, about 1 hour.

Pick off and discard the spices. Use a large spoon to scrape the flesh from the squash and pumpkin into a blender; discard the skins. Strain all the pan juices through a fine-mesh sieve into the blender. Add the stock and puree until very smooth, adding more stock for a thinner soup if desired. Season with salt and pepper.

Strain through a fine-mesh sieve, divide among serving bowls, and drizzle with oil.

SPRING PEA SOUP

The bright spritziness of a dry white vinho verde brings out the sweetness in fresh spring peas, as does the combination of mint and lemon thyme.

SERVES 4

kosher salt	as needed
peas	4 cups (480 g), shelled fresh or thawed frozen
asparagus spears	20 thin, trimmed, tips cut off and reserved, stalks thinly sliced
extra-virgin olive oil	as needed
white onion	½ small, thinly sliced
garlic cloves	5, thinly sliced
dry white vinho verde	½ cup (120 ml)
fresh mint leaves	½ cup (15 g)
Vegetable Stock (page 226)	2½ cups (600 ml), hot
fresh lemon thyme leaves	1 teaspoon
fleur de sel	to taste

Fill a large bowl with ice and water. Bring a large saucepan of water to a boil and salt generously. If you're using fresh peas, add and cook, stirring occasionally, until bright green and crisp-tender, about 5 minutes. Immediately transfer to the ice water. When cool, drain well. Repeat with the asparagus stalks, cooking for 2 minutes. Reserve both separately.

Heat an 8-quart (7.5-L) saucepot over medium-low heat. Coat the bottom with oil, then add the onion and garlic. Season with salt and sweat, stirring occasionally, until the onions are tender, about 10 minutes. Add the vinho verde and boil, stirring occasionally, until evaporated. Add the thawed frozen or blanched fresh peas, asparagus stalks, and mint and cook, stirring, until the peas are bright green, about 3 minutes. Add the stock, season with salt, and remove from the heat. Transfer the mixture to a blender and puree until very smooth. Return to the pot, season with salt, and keep warm over low heat.

Heat 2 teaspoons oil in a medium skillet over medium-high heat. Add the asparagus tips and a pinch of salt and pepper. Cook, tossing, until heated through, about 1 minute. Toss in the thyme. Divide the asparagus tips among serving bowls, then pour in the hot soup. Drizzle with oil and sprinkle with fleur de sel.

MUSSEL SOUP

Shellfish and cured pork are a common Portuguese combination. Mussels and chouriço come together here in a creamy soup finished with an aromatic coconut sauce.

SERVES 4

SPECIAL EQUIPMENT:
> SIPHON WITH ONE N$_2$O CHARGE

SOUP BASE

extra-virgin olive oil	2 tablespoons plus 1 teaspoon
celery stalk	1 small, thinly sliced
white onion	½ small, thinly sliced
garlic cloves	3, thinly sliced
fresh ginger	1 (1-inch/2.5-cm) piece (½ ounce/15 g), peeled and thinly sliced
fresh lemongrass stalk	½, minced
fresh Kaffir lime leaves	2, thinly sliced
fresh bay leaf	1, notches torn every ½ inch (12 mm)
kosher salt	to taste
saffron threads	1 teaspoon
dry Chardonnay	½ cup (120 ml)
Pernod	½ cup (120 ml)
Prince Edward Island mussels	3 pounds 6 ounces (1.5 kg), scrubbed well, beards removed
Chicken Stock (page 226)	as needed, hot
heavy cream	1⅓ cups (315 ml)
fresh parsley	1 small bunch
fresh lemon thyme	1 small bunch

MAKE THE SOUP BASE: Heat the oil in a large saucepot over medium heat. Add the celery, onion, garlic, ginger, lemongrass, lime leaves, bay leaf, and a big pinch of salt. Cook, stirring occasionally, until the onions are just translucent, about 7 minutes. Stir in the saffron.

Add the Chardonnay, bring to a boil, and simmer until the liquid evaporates. Do the same with the Pernod. Stir in the mussels, then add enough chicken stock to cover the mussels by ½ inch (12 mm). Raise the heat to high, cover the pot, and cook until the mussels open, about 5 minutes. With a slotted spoon, remove the mussels. Shell and reserve 16 for serving; save the remaining mussels for another use or serve them alongside the soup. Discard any that do not open.

Simmer the cooking liquid until reduced by one-third, then stir in the cream. Add the parsley and thyme and remove from the heat. Let steep for 15 minutes.

CONTINUED >>

GARNISH

kosher salt	as needed
Yukon gold potatoes	4 small, peeled and cut into 1-inch (2.5-cm) cubes
fennel bulbs	4 small, cored and cut into 1-inch (2.5-cm) cubes
baguette	1 small, cut into 8 (½-inch-/12-mm-thick) slices
extra-virgin olive oil	as needed
cured chouriço	20 (¼-inch-/6-mm-thick) slices
Coconut Sauce (page 67)	1 cup (240 ml)

MAKE THE GARNISH: While the soup base steeps, prepare the garnish. Fill a large bowl with ice and water. Heat a medium saucepan of water to boiling. Very generously salt the water and add the potatoes. Cook, stirring gently, until tender but still holding their shape, about 10 minutes. Use a slotted spoon to transfer the potatoes to the ice water. Do the same with the fennel, cooking until just tender, about 5 minutes, then shocking in the ice water.

Drizzle the baguette slices with oil and broil or toast until just golden brown and crisp.

Lightly coat a large skillet with oil and heat over medium heat. Add the chouriço and cook, turning, until the oil just turns orange and the chouriço is a bit softer. Transfer to a dish.

To assemble the soup, strain the steeped soup base through a fine-mesh sieve into a medium saucepan. Gently heat until very hot. Place the coconut sauce in a siphon with one N_2O charge. Shake well and pipe a mound of coconut mousse in each soup dish. Scatter the potatoes, fennel, baguette, chouriço, and reserved mussels around the mousse, then pour the hot soup over.

MUSSEL SOUP

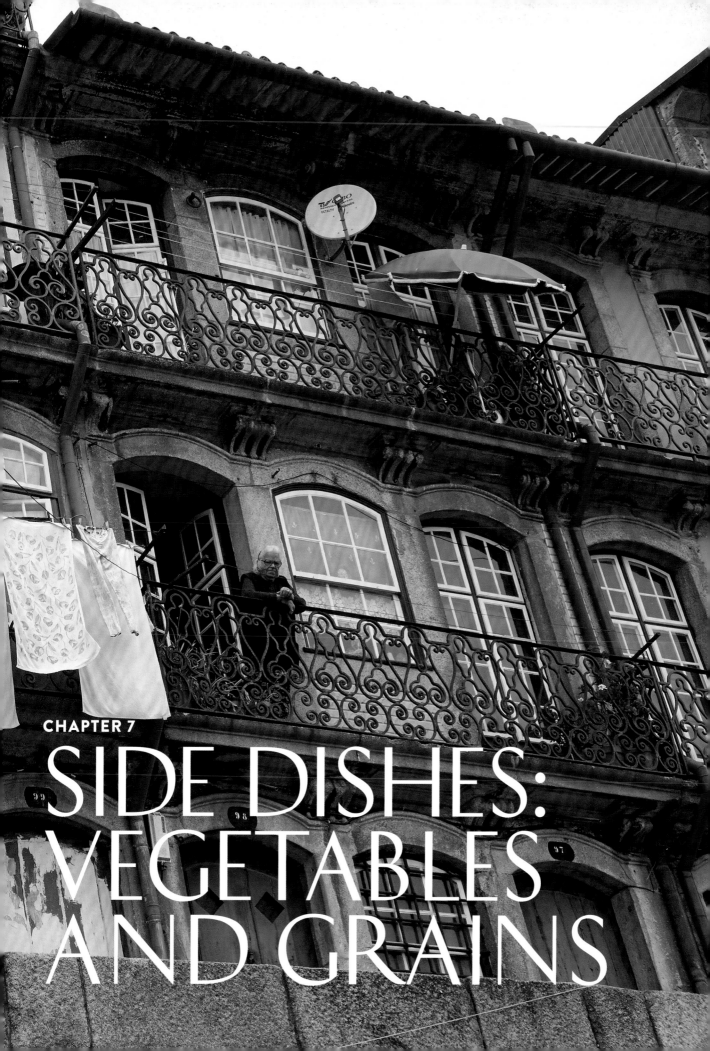

CHAPTER 7

SIDE DISHES: VEGETABLES AND GRAINS

FAVA BEANS WITH MORCELLA AND MINT

Miguel Vaz, the chef at the stunning eco-winery Herdade do Esporão, took me to O Chico, the small-town linoleum-floored Alentejo eatery where he and fellow local chefs go to share beers and hearty home-style food after a busy night of service. This dish is inspired by O Chico's fava bean prepartion. Here, I've kept the beautiful pale green and tender sweetness of fresh favas. The morcella adds plenty of meaty richness to the barely cooked spring vegetables.

SERVES 4

kosher salt	as needed
shucked and shelled fava beans	1½ cups (180 g)
smoked slab bacon, preferably Benton's	2 ounces (55 g), diced
morcella sausage	2 ounces (55 g), cut into ⅓-inch (8-mm) half-moons
extra-virgin olive oil	as needed
Refogado (page 235)	1 tablespoon
fresh oregano leaves	1 tablespoon, finely chopped
lemon	1
fleur de sel	for serving

Fill a large bowl with ice and water. Bring a large saucepan of water to a boil and salt generously. Add the fava beans and cook, stirring occasionally, until bright green and crisp-tender, about 3 minutes. Immediately transfer to the ice water. When cool, drain well.

Cook the bacon in a large sauté pan over medium-high heat, rubbing it around the pan to render the fat, about 7 minutes. Transfer the bacon to paper towels to drain and reserve. Add the morcella to the fat in the pan. Cook, stirring occasionally, until browned. Transfer to paper towels to drain.

Drain the meat fat from the pan and add enough oil to lightly coat the bottom. Reduce the heat to medium and add the refogado. Cook, stirring, until fragrant, about 1 minute.

Remove from the heat and fold in the fava beans, bacon, and morcella until well mixed. Top with the oregano, zest a quarter of the lemon over the mixture, sprinkle with fleur de sel, and drizzle with oil.

GREEN BEANS WITH PEACHES AND ALMONDS

This is an homage to Alain Passard, legendary chef of L'Arpège in Paris, whose way with vegetables changed the way I cook. This sauté celebrates the summer bounty; use the best pole beans and stone fruits you can find at the farmers' market.

SERVES 4

kosher salt and freshly ground white pepper	to taste
green beans	12 ounces (340 g), tipped and tailed, halved at an angle
extra-virgin olive oil	1 tablespoon, plus more to taste
unsalted butter	1 tablespoon
sliced almonds	¼ cup (30 g), toasted
almond oil	to taste
yellow peach	1 medium, pitted and cut into ¼-inch (6-mm) wedges
fresh baby basil leaves	2 teaspoons
fresh marjoram leaves	1 teaspoon
fleur de sel	to taste
Basil Oil (page 239; optional)	to taste

Fill a large bowl with ice and water. Bring a large saucepan of water to a boil and salt generously. Add the beans and cook, stirring occasionally, until bright green and crisp-tender, about 5 minutes. Immediately transfer to the ice water. When cool, drain well. You want the beans completely dry.

Heat a large skillet over medium heat. Add the olive oil and butter and swirl to melt the butter. When the butter foams, add the beans, season with salt and pepper, and toss well. Add the almonds and cook, tossing, for 1 minute. Drizzle in almond oil and toss to coat well, then toss in the peach wedges. Cook to just warm through, about 30 seconds. Transfer to a serving plate.

Sprinkle the basil, marjoram, and fleur de sel on top, then drop some basil oil all around, if using. Otherwise, drizzle on a little more olive oil. Serve immediately.

ZUCCHINI AND SQUASH WITH COCONUT SAUCE

Mild summer squashes can take a lot of flavor while keeping their fresh bite. I float them in an aromatic, creamy coconut sauce, which would taste great with just about any vegetable.

SERVES 4

extra-virgin olive oil	1 tablespoon, plus more to taste
onion	⅓ cup (40 g), thinly sliced
garlic	2 tablespoons thinly sliced
peeled fresh ginger	2 tablespoons thinly sliced
fresh bay leaf	1, notches torn every ½ inch (12 mm)
lemongrass	½ stalk, smashed and thinly sliced at an angle
Kaffir lime leaves	2, thinly sliced
kosher salt	as needed
coconut milk	1 (13.5-ounce/400-ml) can
baby zucchini and summer squashes	8, trimmed and quartered lengthwise
fresh cilantro leaves	¼ cup (7 g)
fresh mint leaves, preferably Vietnamese	2 tablespoons sliced
fleur de sel	for serving
shrimp powder (optional; see Note)	for serving
lime	1, for serving

Heat a large saucepan over medium heat. Add the oil, then the onion, garlic, ginger, bay leaf, lemongrass, and lime leaves. Season generously with salt and sweat, stirring occasionally, until the onion is just tender and transparent, about 5 minutes. Stir in the coconut milk, bring to a boil, then reduce the heat to simmer for 30 minutes.

Meanwhile, fill a large bowl with ice and water. Bring a large saucepan of water to a boil and salt generously. Add the squashes and cook, stirring occasionally, until bright and crisp-tender, about 2 minutes. Immediately transfer to the ice water. When cool, drain well and transfer to a serving dish.

Strain the sauce through a fine-mesh sieve, pressing on the solids to extract as much liquid as possible. Season with salt, then pour over the squash. Sprinkle with the cilantro, mint, fleur de sel, and shrimp powder, if using. Drizzle with oil, then zest the lime directly over the mixture. Cut the lime and squeeze the juice on top to taste. Serve immediately.

NOTE *Shrimp powder makes a world of a difference in this dish, adding a hit of umami at the end. It brings another dimension of flavor and opens up all of the richness in the coconut sauce. I prefer the Maesri brand, but look for any shrimp powder in Asian markets. The only ingredients should be dried shrimp, salt, and sugar (and possibly cornstarch).*

GOAN EGGPLANT CURRY

I love the nice little heat of ginger in this because it's so fresh and vibrant. To keep the spices bright too, I add them late in the process. The eggplant, which I caramelize in a hot pan, makes a good sponge for soaking up this sauce. Even though this would make a great vegetarian entrée, it's also fantastic as a side dish to lamb or baby goat. And beer is a must.

SERVES 4

tomato	1 small, coarsely chopped
strained tomatoes, preferably Pomi	½ cup (120 ml)
unsweetened coconut flakes	½ cup (40 g), toasted
tamarind paste (see Note)	2 tablespoons
extra-virgin olive oil	as needed
white onion	1 medium, very finely chopped
garlic cloves	15, minced
fresh ginger	5-inch (12-cm) piece, peeled and minced
fresh bay leaf	1, notches torn every ½ inch (12 mm)
kosher salt	as needed
coconut milk	1 (13.5-ounce/400-ml) can
globe eggplants	2 large, trimmed and cut into 1-inch (2.5-cm) cubes
Goan Spice Mix (page 233)	1 tablespoon
lime	1, for serving
fresh cilantro leaves	for serving

In a food processor, pulse the tomato, strained tomatoes, coconut flakes, tamarind, and 1 cup (240 ml) water until the solids are finely chopped.

Heat an 8-quart (7.5-L) saucepot over medium heat. Add enough oil to very generously coat the bottom, then add the onion, garlic, ginger, and bay leaf. Season with salt and sweat, stirring occasionally, until the onion is tender, about 10 minutes.

Add enough oil to cover the onion mixture, then add the tomato-coconut paste. Be careful; it'll splatter. Simmer, stirring and scraping the pot frequently, until thickened, about 7 minutes. Stir in the coconut milk and ½ cup (120 ml) water. Season with salt. Gently simmer, stirring occasionally, for 20 minutes.

Meanwhile, heat a large skillet over high heat until very hot. Coat the bottom with oil and add a single layer of eggplant cubes, leaving about 1 inch (2.5 cm) between the pieces. Generously salt and cook, stirring and tossing vigorously, unti golden and browned in spots, about 3 minutes. Transfer to a plate. Repeat with the remaining eggplant.

Fold the eggplant and spice mix into the sauce and simmer, gently stirring occasionally, until the eggplant is tender and the sauce thickens enough to coat the eggplant, about 7 minutes. Discard the bay leaf. Season with salt, then zest the lime directly over the mixture and squeeze in the juice to taste. Garnish with the cilantro and serve hot.

NOTE *If you can only find "wet tamarind," or tamarind still with its seeds, cover ¼ cup in hot water and knead to form a paste. Press the paste through a medium-mesh sieve and scrape the pulp off the strainer. You want 2 tablespoons pulp; discard the seeds.*

COCONUT-SAFFRON CAULIFLOWER AND BROCCOLI

Though it's not immediately apparent, coconut and saffron pair well. In this dish, they elevate humble fall vegetables with layers of heat and spice. The rich sauce also tastes good with tender sweet potatoes.

SERVES 4

coriander seeds	1½ teaspoons
cumin seeds	2½ teaspoons
saffron threads	1½ teaspoons
kosher salt	as needed
cauliflower florets	1 pound (455 g)
broccoli florets	1 pound (455 g)
extra-virgin olive oil	as needed
white onion	1 small, finely diced
garlic cloves	4, minced
fresh bay leaves	2, notches torn every ½ inch (12 mm)
tamarind paste (see Note, page 170)	3 tablespoons
coconut milk	2 (13.5-ounce/400-ml) cans
jalapeño	1 large, stemmed, seeded, and minced
crushed red chile flakes	for serving
fresh lime juice	for serving
fresh cilantro leaves	for serving

In a small skillet, heat the coriander, cumin, and saffron over medium heat, tossing occasionally, until toasted and fragrant. Let cool completely, then grind in a spice grinder until coarsely ground, with a few broken coriander husks remaining.

Fill a large bowl with ice and water. Bring a large saucepan of water to a boil and salt generously. Add the cauliflower and cook, stirring occasionally, until crisp-tender, about 5 minutes. Immediately transfer to the ice water. When cool, drain well. Repeat the blanching and shocking with the broccoli.

Heat an 8-quart (7.5-L) saucepot over medium heat. Add enough oil to very generously coat the bottom, then add the onion, garlic, and bay leaves. Season with salt and sweat, stirring occasionally, until the onion is tender, about 10 minutes. Stir in the tamarind paste and toasted spices and cook, stirring, for 1 minute. Stir in the coconut milk and 1 cup (240 ml) water. Season with salt. Simmer, stirring occasionally, until thickened, about 35 minutes.

Stir in the cauliflower, broccoli, and jalapeño. Simmer, stirring occasionally, until the cauliflower and broccoli are just tender, about 5 minutes. Discard the bay leaves. Season with salt, chile flakes, and lime juice. Top with cilantro and serve hot.

COCONUT-SAFFRON CAULIFLOWER AND BROCCOLI

VINEGARED KALE PUREE

ESPERRAGADO

Throughout Portugal, home cooks make a version of this tangy textured puree with whichever dark leafy greens look best at the market: spinach, turnip greens, and other regional varieties. By chopping the leaves after cooking them, you get a consistency that's like the Platonic ideal of creamed spinach, with a bright, clean lightness. The vinegar discolors the greens, so drizzle it on right before serving.

SERVES 4

kosher salt and freshly ground white pepper	as needed
kale	2 bunches (8 ounces/224 g), stems and tough ribs removed
extra-virgin olive oil	5 tablespoons, plus more to taste
white onion	1 small, halved and thinly sliced
garlic cloves	6, thinly sliced crosswise
sherry vinegar	2 tablespoons, plus more to taste

Fill a large bowl with ice and water. Heat a large saucepot of water to a boil and salt generously. Add a handful of the kale leaves. Cook, stirring gently, until bright green and soft, about 5 minutes. Use a slotted spoon to transfer the kale to the ice water. When it's cool, transfer to a colander to drain. Bring the water back to a boil and repeat, cooking a handful of kale at a time. You have to work in batches. Otherwise, the water will lose its boil and the kale will turn brown before it cooks. Reserve the kale cooking water.

Once all the kale is drained, use your hands to squeeze out as much water as possible. Coarsely chop the leaves.

Meanwhile, heat ¼ cup (60 ml) oil in a large saucepan over medium-low heat. Add the onion, garlic, and a big pinch of salt. Cook, stirring occasionally, until the onion is tender with no color. Go slow and long here, about 20 minutes. Add the chopped kale and stir until it's heated through.

Transfer the kale to a blender or food processor along with 1 tablespoon each of oil and the kale cooking water. Pulse until very finely chopped, adding a little more cooking water if needed to get the machine going. You want the mixture to be quite dry and with some texture still in the leaves.

Season with salt and pepper. Right when you're ready to serve, drizzle with the vinegar and oil. Stir to mix in the seasonings and taste and adjust the salt, pepper, vinegar, and oil. Serve immediately.

BROCCOLI RAAB WITH GARLIC AND RED CHILE FLAKES

Growing up, we often ate garlicky sautéed grelos at home and in Portugal. They're fragrant spring greens with coiled tops like fiddleheads and pale stalks like turnip greens. They're the young shoots of broccoli that don't grow heads and broccoli raab is a close substitute. We always had it with seared salt cod (page 34), but it's great with any fish dish.

SERVES 4

kosher salt and freshly ground black pepper as needed
broccoli raab 1 large bunch (8 ounces/224 g), trimmed
extra-virgin olive oil 3 tablespoons
garlic cloves 4 large, minced
crushed red chile flakes pinch, or to taste

Fill a large bowl with ice and water. Heat a large saucepot of water to a boil and salt generously. Add a handful of the broccoli raab. Cook, stirring gently, until bright green and soft, about 1 minute. Transfer to the ice water. When cool, transfer to paper towels to drain. Bring the water back to a boil and repeat, cooking a handful of broccoli raab at a time. You have to work in batches. Otherwise, the water will lose its boil and the broccoli raab won't stay crisp.

In a large skillet, heat the oil over medium-low heat. Add the garlic and sweat, stirring occasionally, until light golden brown, about 2 minutes. Add the chile flakes and toast, stirring, until fragrant, about 30 seconds. Add the broccoli raab, season with salt and pepper, and cook, tossing, until crisp-tender, about 3 minutes.

BRUSSELS SPROUTS WITH QUINCE AND BACON

In early fall, I like to make the most of the short quince season. The fuzzy, squat, pear-shaped fruit tastes great with savory, smoky bacon and earthy Brussels sprouts.

SERVES 4

sugar	1 cup (200 g)
kosher salt	as needed
quince	1, peeled, quartered, and cored
Brussels sprouts	4 cups (350 g), cored and leaves separated
smoked slab bacon, preferably Benton's	2 ounces (55 g), cut into ½-inch (12-mm) cubes
fresh thyme leaves	¼ teaspoon
Maldon sea salt	to taste
lemon wedges	for serving

In a small saucepan, combine the sugar with 2 cups (480 ml) water. Bring to a boil, stirring to dissolve the sugar, then reduce the heat to simmer. Add the quince, cover, and simmer gently until just tender, about 15 minutes. You want the quince to be soft but not mushy; it should still hold its shape. Transfer to a cutting board with a slotted spoon, let cool, and cut into ⅓-inch (8-mm) dice. Reserve the simple syrup for another use.

Meanwhile, fill a large bowl with ice and water. Heat a large saucepot of water to a boil and salt generously with kosher salt. Add the Brussels sprouts leaves. Cook, stirring gently, until bright green, about 1 minute. Drain and transfer to the ice water. When cool, transfer to paper towels to drain well.

In a large sauté pan, cook the bacon over medium-low heat, stirring occasionally, until the fat renders, about 7 minutes. Raise the heat to high and add the Brussels sprouts leaves. Cook, tossing, until the leaves brown in spots, about 1 minute. Remove from the heat and toss in the diced quince.

Transfer to a serving dish and sprinkle with the thyme. Lightly season with Maldon salt and squeeze lemon juice on top right before serving.

SMOKED BABY BEETS

Meaty and sweet, beets take well to a little smoke. I initially prepared these to pair with the Baby Goat Terrine (page 139), but they're delicious with other meat dishes too.

SERVES 10

SPECIAL EQUIPMENT:
> SMOKER

baby red beets	4 bunches (3 pounds/1.3 g)
extra-virgin olive oil	¼ cup (60 ml), plus more to taste
kosher salt and freshly ground white pepper	to taste
Chicken Stock (page 226)	1 cup (240 ml)
unsalted butter	¼ cup (55 g), cut into cubes
applewood smoking chips	as needed
apple balsamic vinegar	to taste

Preheat the oven to 375°F (190°C). Trim all but ½ inch (12 mm) of the stems from the beets. Scrub well. Place the beets in a roasting pan, drizzle with the oil, and season with salt and pepper. Add the stock and butter and cover tightly with foil. Bake until a cake tester pierces the beets with no resistance, 45 minutes to 1 hour. Meanwhile, prepare a smoker with the applewood smoking chips.

Uncover and remove the beets from the pan. Transfer the beets to the smoker and smoke for 10 minutes. When cool enough to handle, use a towel to rub the peels off the beets. Quarter the beets and transfer to a bowl. Toss with vinegar, oil, salt, and pepper.

SWEET CARROT CUSTARDS

With their natural sugars, carrots make a great base for creamy custard. I steam these in cylinder molds, but any 4-ounce (120-ml) mold works too. These silky, delicate custards complement mild game, such as venison (page 134).

SERVES 4

unsalted butter	1 tablespoon
carrots	10 ounces (280 g), peeled and thinly sliced
skim milk	⅔ cup (165 ml)
sugar	1 tablespoon plus 1 teaspoon
egg yolk	1 large
kosher salt and freshly ground white pepper	to taste
agar agar	¾ teaspoon
locust bean gum (optional; see Note)	pinch

Melt the butter in a medium saucepan over medium-low heat. Stir in the carrots, cover with a parchment-paper lid, and sweat, stirring occasionally, until softened, 10 to 15 minutes. Uncover, add the milk, and bring to a simmer. Cover with the parchment lid and cook at a slow simmer until a cake tester pierces the carrots with no resistance. Strain, reserving the carrots and their cooking liquid separately.

Combine the carrots, sugar, and egg yolk in a blender. Puree until smooth. Season with salt and pepper.

In a small saucepan, stir the agar agar and locust bean gum (if using) into the reserved carrot cooking liquid. Cook over low heat for 3 minutes. Pour into the carrot mixture and blend until smooth. Press through a fine-mesh sieve.

Transfer the mixture to a piping bag. Pipe ½ cup (120 ml) into a 1-inch (2.5-cm) cylindrical tube or other mold. Repeat three times. Steam the molds over simmering water until the custards are heated through, about 4 minutes. Unmold and serve.

NOTE *Locust bean gum, available in professional kitchen supply stores, helps to really set these custards, though the agar agar also sets them sufficiently.*

WILD MUSHROOMS WITH BRUSSELS SPROUTS

Throughout the forests of northern Portugal, home cooks forage for wild mushrooms all fall, the way they have for centuries. In New York City, I do the same in the jungle of the Union Square Greenmarket. A hint of citrus in the lemon thyme balances the deep earthiness of the mushrooms.

SERVES 4

kosher salt and freshly ground black pepper	to taste
Brussels sprouts leaves	¼ cup (20 g)
extra-virgin olive oil	as needed
black trumpet mushrooms	1 cup (55 g), trimmed, cleaned, and dried
small chanterelle mushrooms	1 cup (55 g), trimmed, cleaned, and dried
fresh lemon thyme leaves	2 teaspoons

Fill a large bowl with ice and water. Bring a large saucepan of water to a boil and salt generously. Add the Brussels sprouts leaves and cook, stirring occasionally, until bright green and crisp-tender, about 1 minute. Immediately transfer to the ice water. When cool, drain well.

Heat a small skillet over medium-high heat. Coat with oil and add the trumpet mushrooms. Cook, tossing occasionally, until light golden brown. Transfer to a dish. Repeat with the chanterelles and transfer to the same dish. Sprinkle with 1 teaspoon of the thyme and season with salt and pepper.

Wipe out the skillet and heat again over medium-high heat. Lightly coat with oil and add the Brussels sprouts leaves. Cook, tossing occasionally, until warmed and bright. Sprinkle with the remaining 1 teaspoon thyme and season with salt and pepper. Lightly fold into the mushrooms and serve immediately.

WHITE BUTTON MUSHROOM STEW

The flavors here, inspired by my mom's signature holiday side dish, are simple and wholesome. But there's a lot of umami from the mushrooms and tomatoes and a rustic smokiness from the chile and paprika.

SERVES 4

white button mushrooms	1 pound (455 g), preferably very small
extra-virgin olive oil	as needed
kosher salt and freshly ground black pepper	to taste
white onion	½ small, very finely diced
garlic cloves	2, minced
fresh bay leaf	1, notches torn every ½ inch (12 mm)
crushed red chile flakes	1½ teaspoons
tomato puree	¾ cup
fresh parsley	1 sprig, plus ¼ cup (7 g) leaves, finely chopped
pimentón (smoked sweet paprika)	¼ teaspoon

Quickly submerge the mushrooms in a bowl of cold water and then lift them out, leaving the grit behind. Use paper towels to dry and rub off any remaining dirt, then trim just the ends of the stems. Unless the mushrooms are very small, quarter or halve them to get ½-inch (12-mm) pieces. Place the mushrooms in a bowl, drizzle with oil, sprinkle with salt, and toss to coat.

Heat a medium saucepan over medium-low heat. Coat the pan with oil, then add the onion, garlic, and bay leaf. Season with salt. You want the onion to be just coated with the oil, so add more if needed. Sweat, constantly stirring and scraping down the sides of the pan to prevent browning, until the onions start to soften, about 3 minutes. Stir in the chile flakes and continue sweating, stirring and scraping often, until the onion is translucent, about 2 minutes.

Stir in the tomato puree and bring to a simmer. Reduce the heat to low and simmer for 10 minutes.

Stir in the mushrooms, parsley sprig, and pimentón until well coated. Bring the mixture to a simmer over medium-low heat, cover, and simmer until the mushrooms are just tender, about 20 minutes. Adjust the heat to maintain a slow bubble; you don't want to cook the mushrooms to death.

For even more flavor, let the mushrooms steep in the mixture off the heat or refrigerate them overnight, then reheat them the next day.

Season with salt and pepper. Discard the bay leaf and parsley sprig, then top with the chopped parsley.

SHIITAKES AND GIROLLES WITH WHEAT BERRIES

Chef Pascal Barbot mentored me while I was doing a stage at L'Arpège in France and inspired me to create this dish. He went on to open his own restaurant, L'Astrance, and created a foie gras–white mushroom dish there. I've gone vegetarian in this version instead, using wheat berries to make this a flavorful entrée or a side dish that works well with a range of meats.

SERVES 4

fresh shiitake caps	6 medium
kosher salt and freshly ground white pepper	to taste
hard red winter wheat berries	1 cup (200 g)
Vegetable Stock (page 226)	3½ cups (840 ml), plus more as needed
unsalted butter	2 teaspoons, plus more as needed
extra-virgin olive oil	to taste
girolles (baby chanterelle mushrooms)	1 cup (55 g)
shallot	1 teaspoon minced
fresh lemon juice	to taste
navel orange	1 medium
fresh lemon thyme leaves	¼ teaspoon, plus more for serving
fresh mint leaves	1 teaspoon, thinly sliced, plus more for serving
fresh basil leaves	1 teaspoon, thinly sliced, plus more for serving
almond oil	¼ teaspoon, plus more for serving
white button mushrooms	8 large, trimmed
Maldon sea salt	for serving

Prepare a dehydrator or preheat the oven to 200°F (90°C), on the convection setting if you have it.

Cut each shiitake cap into ¼-inch (6-mm) slices at a 45-degree angle. In a large bowl, toss them with a very generous pinch of kosher salt. Arrange in a single layer in the dehydrator or on a wire rack set in a half sheet pan for the oven. Turn on the dehydrator or bake until the shiitakes are completely dry, thin, and crisp. The timing on this will range depending on your dehydrator; it'll take 8 hours to overnight in the oven. Check the pieces occasionally. They're ready if they crack and break when you bend them. Cool the shiitakes completely, then grind to a powder in a spice grinder.

Meanwhile, place the wheat berries in a medium bowl and add enough cold water to cover by 1 inch (2.5 cm). Cover and refrigerate overnight. This soaking step will help them cook.

Drain the wheat berries, rinse, and drain again. Transfer to a medium saucepan, along with the stock and 2 tablespoons salt. Stir well, then bring to a boil. Reduce the heat to simmer until tender, about 40 minutes. Drain and spread out in a single layer on a half sheet pan to cool.

Heat a medium sauté pan over medium-high heat. Add the butter and 2 teaspoons olive oil. When the butter melts, add the girolles and a generous pinch of kosher salt. Cook, tossing, for 1 minute, then add the shallot. Continue cooking until the mushrooms are lightly browned and the shallot is translucent, about 1 minute. Remove from the heat and sprinkle with lemon juice to taste.

Finely grate ½ teaspoon zest from the orange and reserve. Cut off the peel and pith from the orange and cut out the segments between the membranes. Cut each segment crosswise into ½-inch (12-mm) pieces.

Heat a large sauté pan over medium heat and add enough olive oil to coat the bottom. When hot, add the wheat berries and cook, shaking and tossing the pan occasionally, until toasted, about 2 minutes. Toss in the girolles and cook, stirring, for 1 minute, then remove from the heat. Fold in the orange zest and segments, lemon thyme, mint, basil, and almond oil. Season with kosher salt and pepper.

Divide the wheat berries and girolles among four serving dishes and drizzle generously with olive oil. Use a mandoline or very sharp knife to cut the button mushrooms into paper-thin slices. Arrange the slices on top of the wheat berries. Drizzle a little almond oil on top of the mushroom slices. Place the shiitake powder in a fine-mesh sieve and dust the white mushrooms with the powder. Drizzle with olive oil and sprinkle with Maldon salt and additional herbs. Serve immediately.

RICE

Some kids wake up to the smell of brewing coffee. In my house, I rose to the aroma of refogado, which is olive oil sizzling with onions, garlic, and tomatoes. Not every day, of course. On the Sunday mornings I got hit with that scent in my sleep, I knew it'd be a good day. It meant we were going to the beach.

My mom would be in the kitchen, stirring rice into the pot before the sun rose; my dad would be there too, packing the coolers with marinated pork steaks, cushioning the Tupperware with ice. My sister and I would help, piling watermelons, charcoal, fishing rods, and beach towels into the back of our GMC Jimmy. I worked as fast as I could to get to the beach early to fish, but we knew we had to wait for my mom's tomato rice. That crucial pot always had to be the last item to load.

We'd hit Route 33 just as the sun cleared the trees and head south from Danbury, our central Connecticut factory town, to the Sherwood Island State Park in tony coastal Westport. As soon as we pulled into the parking lot, I'd run down the huge hill that led to the water, rod in hand. By eight o'clock, I'd have surf-cast my first line of the day with my cousin Alex. We'd mess around with our bait, hoping for some baby bluefish to throw on the grill, while my uncle picked mussels off the rocks.

My mom and aunt would set the picnic table with a floral tablecloth, paper plates, and silverware—always real silverware. My dad would get the grill going and start cutting up the melons, right on the table. We'd all sit, sandy from the beach, and pass the platters of charred meat, crisp green salad, and, of course, that tomato rice.

My mom actually made tomato rice all the time, but it never tasted better than on the beach. The chewy grains were suspended in an intense tomato base, made with the fruit from our garden. The rice itself, however, was Uncle Ben's. Those orange packages were a staple in our pantry. When I first recreated my family's tomato rice recipe for this book, I thought that maybe Uncle Ben's rice would taste great. Maybe it was the secret to the dish; I'm not such a food snob that I wouldn't at least try it.

Turns out it's not the key to this dish. My parents relied on it because there weren't other options at the market. Back in Portugal, they had their pick of grains, harvested from the paddies along the western coast. More than other Western European countries, Portugal grows and uses rice extensively. Short-grained carolino is a common variety, not to be confused with American long-grained Carolina. Not only does carolino have a nice chew, it also soaks up the liquid it's cooking in like a sponge, making for deeply flavorful dishes. Because it's difficult to find here, I use the more commonly available cebolla, bomba, and calasparra grains from Spain.

On a recent trip to Portugal, I tasted some long-grain rice dishes that blew me away too. At Cervejaria da Esquina in Lisbon, the chef did a killer seafood rice. The broth combined the intensity of a great shellfish stock with a light creaminess from the al dente rice. In Porto, I had a simple side of fragrant saffron rice that was light and fluffy. There, the cooks used basmati. When I cruised the aisles of local supermarkets, I found a range of grains from short to long. I've been experimenting with different rice dishes since, playing with the traditional versions by mixing up the grains and intensifying the seasonings. Even though I don't use the brand of grains I grew up eating, I think I've caught the comforting deliciousness of my mom's tomato rice.

My mom and aunt Natalia grilling meat for a family cookout.

TOMATO RICE

beefsteak tomatoes	8 large ripe
kosher salt and freshly	
ground white pepper	as needed
tomato paste	1 tablespoon
fresh bay leaf	1, notches torn every ½ inch (12 mm)
extra-virgin olive oil	as needed
Refogado (page 235)	3 tablespoons
cebolla rice	2 cups (430 g)
fresh parsley leaves	1 cup (28 g), very finely chopped

The most important step in this classic recipe is buying really ripe tomatoes. Better yet, pluck them from your garden if you've grown them. There are layers of tomato flavor here—from the "stock" of tomato water to the sautéed dice scattered throughout the rice. I love this on its own or with a nice piece of grilled fish.

SERVES 4 TO 6

Fill a large bowl with ice and water. Bring a large saucepan of water to a boil. Slit an "x" in the base of two of the tomatoes and drop in the boiling water. Let sit for 10 seconds, then transfer to the ice water. Drain and remove and discard the skins. Transfer the seeds to a blender; cut the flesh into a ¼-inch (6-mm) dice and refrigerate in an airtight container until ready to use.

Coarsely chop the remaining six tomatoes and add to the blender along with a generous pinch of salt. Puree until very smooth. Set a large sieve over a large bowl and line with a clean kitchen towel. Pour the tomato puree into the towel, cover, and refrigerate overnight. The liquids will strain through. You need 4½ cups (1 L) tomato water.

Preheat the oven to 375°F (190°C).

Heat a large skillet over medium heat. Add the reserved diced tomatoes and a generous pinch of salt. Cook, stirring occasionally, until the excess moisture evaporates, about 3 minutes. Add the tomato paste, bay leaf, and enough oil to make the mixture sizzle. Cook, stirring gently, until the mixture looks concentrated, about 3 minutes. Remove from the heat.

Heat an ovenproof 12-inch (30.5-cm) paella or sauté pan or Dutch oven over medium heat. Add enough oil to generously coat the bottom, then add the refogado. Cook, stirring, for 1 minute. Add the rice and 1 tablespoon oil. Continue stirring until the rice is toasted and hot to the touch, about 2 minutes. Stir in half of the tomato mixture and spread the rice evenly in the pan. Let it cook for 2 minutes, then gently stir in 2 cups (480 ml) of the tomato water and a generous pinch of salt. Spread in an even layer and adjust the heat to maintain a steady simmer. Cook, without stirring, for 5 minutes. Gently stir in 2 cups (480 ml) more tomato water, scraping up any rice stuck to the bottom of the pan. Season with salt. Spread in an even layer and simmer until the rice is almost al dente, about 15 minutes. You don't want to stir the rice and release its starches; that will make the rice gummy.

Pour the remaining ½ cup (120 ml) tomato water into the rice. Transfer to the oven and bake until the rice is al dente, a light brown crust has formed on the bottom, and the tomato liquid is creamy, about 20 minutes. Remove from the oven and let rest for a few minutes. Discard the bay leaf. Sprinkle with parsley and serve.

AROMATIC BLACK-EYED PEAS

In recent years, I've connected with Southern American cuisine through friendships with chefs like Sean Brock and Mike Lata in Charleston, South Carolina, and Sam Beall and Joseph Lenn at Blackberry Farm in the mountains of Tennessee. They share a certain soulfulness with Portuguese chefs, so I've adopted one of their native beans for an Iberian-inspired octopus salad (page 63).

MAKES ABOUT 4 CUPS (660 G)

dried black-eyed peas	2 cups (400 g)
coriander seeds	1 tablespoon
whole black peppercorns	1 tablespoon
fresh parsley	1 small bunch
fresh thyme	1 small bunch
Vegetable Stock (page 226)	6 cups (1.4 L), cold, plus more as needed
carrot	1 large, peeled and halved lengthwise
celery stalk	1 large
white onion	½ large
garlic	1 whole head, cut crosswise in half
smoked slab bacon, preferably Benton's	1 (2-by-1-inch/5-by-2.5-cm) slab
kosher salt	to taste
extra-virgin olive oil	as needed

In a large bowl, cover the black-eyed peas with cold water by 2 inches (5 cm). Let soak overnight. The next day, drain, rinse, and drain again.

Wrap the coriander, peppercorns, parsley, and thyme in a piece of cheesecloth and tie with kitchen twine. To a large saucepot, add the stock, carrot, celery, onion, garlic, bacon, black-eyed peas, and herb sachet. The stock should cover everything by at least 1 inch (2.5 cm). If it doesn't, add more. Cover with a piece of parchment paper cut the same diameter as the pot.

Bring to a simmer over medium-low heat, but don't let the liquid boil. If it does, the peas will burst. Simmer low and slow until the peas are just starting to become tender, about 45 minutes. Season very generously with salt. Keep cooking until the peas are tender, about 45 minutes longer.

Discard the onion, garlic, carrot, celery, bacon, and herb sachet. Let the peas cool to room temperature in their cooking liquid. If using immediately, drain the peas; reserve the liquid for another use. Toss with enough oil to coat. Otherwise, cover tightly and refrigerate the peas in their cooking liquid until cold or for up to 5 days. Drain and toss with oil before eating or using in other dishes.

BACON-BRAISED CHICKPEAS

Chickpeas, among other beans, are essential to the hearty regional cuisine of the Alentejo in Portugal. I like to pair the meaty beans with cured pork, another regional staple, and to serve these with salt cod in a salad (page 39).

SERVES 4

dried chickpeas	1 cup (200 g)
coriander seeds	1½ teaspoons
whole black peppercorns	1½ teaspoons
fresh bay leaf	1, notches torn every ½ inch (12 mm)
fresh thyme	3 sprigs
onion	½ small
whole cloves	2
smoked slab bacon, preferably Benton's	1 (6-by-1-inch/15-by-2.5-cm) slab
Vegetable Stock (page 226)	3 cups (720 ml), cold, plus more as needed
carrot	1 small, peeled and halved lengthwise
celery stalk	1 small
kosher salt	to taste

In a large bowl, cover the chickpeas with cold water by 2 inches (5 cm). Let soak overnight. The next day, drain, rinse, and drain again.

Wrap the coriander, peppercorns, bay leaf, and thyme in a piece of cheesecloth and tie with kitchen twine. Stud the onion with the cloves. In a large saucepot, combine the bacon, stock, chickpeas, carrot, celery, herb sachet, and onion. The stock should cover everything by at least 1 inch (2.5 cm). If it doesn't, add more.

Bring to a simmer over medium-low heat, then simmer low and slow until the chickpeas are tender, about 1½ hours. Season very generously with salt. Keep cooking until the chickpeas are very, very soft and almost falling apart but still holding their shape, about 30 minutes longer. The chickpeas will firm up when they cool; that's why it's so important to get them really tender now.

Discard the carrot, celery, onion, bacon, and herb sachet. Let the chickpeas cool to room temperature in their cooking liquid, then cover tightly and refrigerate in their cooking liquid until cold, at least 3 hours or for up to 5 days. Drain before eating or using in other dishes.

CAULIFLOWER AND BACON MIGAS

Migas are an Alentejo specialty that makes the most of leftover bread by soaking it in meat juices. There are a million different versions of the dish out there, and I decided to lighten the classic hearty version by adding earthy cauliflower and using vegetable stock instead of meat broth. To get a rich meatiness in this side dish, I cook it all in bacon fat, then serve it with the browned chunks of meat.

SERVES 4

kosher salt and freshly ground white pepper	to taste
cauliflower florets	¾ cup (80 g)
extra-virgin olive oil	as needed
smoked slab bacon, preferably Benton's	4 (1-inch-/2.5-cm-square) pieces
Refogado (page 235)	1 tablespoon
day-old country bread cubes	2¼ cups (63 g) ½-inch (12-mm) cubes, toasted
Vegetable Stock (page 226)	4½ cups (1 L), plus more as needed
lemon	1
fresh lemon thyme leaves	¼ teaspoon
fresh cilantro leaves	1 tablespoon, thinly sliced

Fill a large bowl with ice and water. Bring a large saucepan of water to a boil and salt generously. Add the cauliflower and cook, stirring occasionally, until just tender, about 5 minutes. Immediately transfer to the ice water. When cool, drain well and cut into ½-inch (12-mm) pieces.

Heat a 4-quart (3.8-L) Dutch oven or casserole over medium heat. Add just enough oil to coat the bottom, then add the bacon. Cook, stirring occasionally, until the fat is rendered and the bacon is lightly browned, about 4 minutes. Transfer the bacon to paper towels to drain; reserve.

Add the refogado to the rendered fat and cook, stirring, until fragrant, about 2 minutes. Fold in the bread, then fold in the stock and drizzle with oil. The bread should be evenly soaked with the stock; add more if needed. Fold in the cauliflower and cook until heated through.

Zest the lemon directly over the mixture, then squeeze in the juice. Season with salt and pepper and top with the thyme and cilantro leaves. Serve with the bacon on the side.

FRIED SHOESTRING
POTATOES

These crunchy thread-thin potatoes top my Bacalhau à Brás (page 31), but they're also an amazing snack on their own or on top of just about anything. You can easily make more. Just be sure to fry them in small batches to keep the potatoes crisp.

MAKES 3 TABLESPOONS

canola oil as needed
Yukon gold potato 1 small

Fill a small saucepan with oil to a depth of 2 inches (5 cm). Bring to 375°F (190°C) over medium-high heat.

While the oil heats, peel the potato, then cut into scant ⅟₁₆-inch (2-mm) slices. Cut each slice into scant ⅟₁₆-inch (2-mm) shoestring batons. Rinse well with cold water; otherwise, excess starch will cause them to clump when frying. Dry well on paper towels.

Add the potatoes in batches to the hot oil to fry until golden brown and crisp, adjusting the heat to maintain the temperature and gently stirring to cook evenly. Drain on paper towels. Use immediately or store in an airtight container for up to 2 hours.

POTATOES CONFIT

Here, savory rendered duck fat infuses tender gold potatoes with an incomparable richness, but I enjoy the olive oil variation just as much.

SERVES 4

coriander seeds	1 tablespoon
whole white peppercorns	1 tablespoon
baby Yukon gold potatoes	1 pound (455 g)
fresh thyme	½ bunch
fresh bay leaves	2, notches torn every ½ inch (12 mm)
kosher salt	1 tablespoon
garlic cloves	4, smashed
rendered duck fat	3 cups (720 ml), plus more as needed

In a small Dutch oven, heat the coriander and peppercorns over medium-low heat, tossing occasionally, until toasted and fragrant. Add the remaining ingredients. The duck fat should cover the potatoes; add more if needed.

Bring the fat to a simmer, then adjust the heat to maintain a slow, steady bubble. Cook until the potatoes are tender, about 20 minutes. A cake tester should slide through one easily.

Let cool slightly in the duck fat and remove with a slotted spoon to serve warm or at room temperature. The fat can be strained through a fine-mesh sieve and used two more times.

VARIATION

POTATOES IN OLIVE OIL CONFIT Omit the coriander seeds. Add 4 sprigs fresh rosemary, cut into 2-inch (5-cm) pieces, along with the thyme and substitute extra-virgin olive oil for the duck fat.

WARM SMASHED POTATOES

BATATAS A MORRO

On every family-style platter in Portugal, whether it's loaded with grilled seafood or meat, smashed disks of potato sit at the bottom, soaking up all the juices. Sometimes they come on the side too, slick with fruity olive oil. Their thin skins crisp and brown after a turn on a hot grill and give way to moist, tender flesh.

SERVES 4

small Yukon gold potatoes	16
garlic cloves	2, smashed
fresh thyme	7 sprigs
fresh rosemary	4 sprigs, snipped into 2-inch (5-cm) pieces
fresh bay leaves	3, notches torn every ½ inch (12 mm)
kosher salt	2 teaspoons
extra-virgin olive oil	as needed
fresh parsley leaves	3 tablespoons, finely chopped
fleur de sel	for serving

Prepare a grill by heating a mixture of all-natural briquettes and hardwood lump charcoal until very hot.

Put the potatoes in a saucepan just big enough to hold them in one layer. They should have enough space to move a little. Add enough water to cover the potatoes, then add the garlic, thyme, rosemary, bay leaves, and kosher salt.

Bring to a simmer over medium heat and cook until the potatoes are soft enough to mush if you press one with your finger, about **30 minutes**. (Watch out—they're hot!) Keep adjusting the heat as you simmer to maintain slow bubbles on the surface. Use a slotted spoon to transfer the potatoes to a plate and let them cool a little. Discard the garlic, herbs, and cooking liquid.

Gently smash each potato to flatten into a thick disk. Lightly coat in oil, then grill, turning once, until charred in spots, about **3 minutes**. Transfer to a large bowl and very gently toss with the parsley and some oil and fleur de sel.

VARIATIONS

SKILLET SMASHED POTATOES You can also finish this in a skillet: Heat a large sauté pan over high heat and coat the bottom with a little oil. Add the smashed potatoes in a single layer and brown, turning once.

RICH SMASHED POTATOES Use Potatoes Confit (page 195), and either grill or sauté them after smashing.

BUTTERED SOUTHERN-STYLE CORNBREAD

Broa, the signature yeasted cornbread of the Minho province, sustained generations with its sturdy density. I prefer cakey American cornbread and created this version to showcase another homeland favorite: butter. I got the most amazing artisanal butter from a farmer in Vermont and wanted to show it off by keeping it out of the batter and letting a generous slab melt into the hot-out-of-the-oven bread. Look for cultured butter with a high fat content, preferably from a local farm.

SERVES 4

coarse yellow cornmeal	1¾ cups (245 g)
kosher salt	1½ teaspoons
sugar	¾ teaspoon
baking powder	¾ teaspoon
baking soda	¾ teaspoon
egg	1 large, at room temperature
buttermilk	2 cups (480 ml)
highest-quality butter	for the pan and for serving
fresh lemon thyme leaves	for serving

Place four (4-inch/10-cm) cast-iron skillets in the oven. Preheat the oven to 375°F (190°C).

In a medium bowl, whisk together the cornmeal, salt, sugar, baking powder, and baking soda to combine. In a large bowl, whisk together the egg and buttermilk until well combined. Add the dry ingredients to the wet and gently whisk just until incorporated.

Carefully swirl a pat of butter in the hot skillets to coat the bottoms and sides, then divide the batter among the skillets.

Bake until golden and set, about 10 minutes. The edges will be browned and pull away from the sides of the pans. Immediately top each bread with a generous pat of butter and a few thyme leaves. Serve hot, with more butter on the side.

NOTE *You can also bake the batter in an 8-inch (20-cm) cast-iron skillet for about 20 minutes.*

PICKLES

I consider pickles a side dish because I love to just snack on them with charcuterie. Of course, I also use them in everything from main dishes to salads. This is my go-to spiced pickling liquid and I constantly experiment with different vegetables and fruits with each season. See the facing page for some of my favorites.

MAKES UP TO 6 CUPS (ABOUT 900 G)

ALL-PURPOSE PICKLING LIQUID

whole black peppercorns	1½ teaspoons
coriander seeds	1½ teaspoons
rice wine vinegar	2 cups (480 ml)
sugar	1½ cups (300 g)
kosher salt	3 tablespoons
fresh bay leaf	1, notches torn every ½ inch (12 mm)

**Pickling Fruit or Vegetables
(amounts follow)**

MAKE THE PICKLING LIQUID: In a small skillet, heat the peppercorns and coriander over medium heat, tossing occasionally, until toasted and fragrant.

In a small saucepan, bring the vinegar and 4 cups (960 ml) water to a boil. Stir in the sugar, salt, bay leaf, and toasted spices. Boil, stirring occasionally, until the sugar and salt dissolve. Remove from the heat and steep for 10 minutes. Strain through a fine-mesh sieve and pour hot over the prepared vegetables or fruits in a nonreactive container. This amount of liquid can pickle up to 6 cups of solids.

Let cool to room temperature, then cover tightly and refrigerate for at least 2 hours or for up to 1 week. The pickling flavors get stronger over time. Strain the pickles and reserve the liquid. You can reuse the same pickling liquid twice.

PICKLING FRUITS OR VEGETABLES

Use some or all of the examples below or experiment with your own produce.

PRODUCE	CUT	PREPARATION
Kirby cucumbers	6, trimmed and cut into ½-inch (12-mm) half-moons	raw
cauliflower	½ small, cut into ½-inch (12-mm) pieces	blanch and shock
carrots	5, peeled and cut into ½-inch (12-mm) pieces	blanch and shock
ramp bulbs	1 bunch, trimmed	raw
shallots	4, peeled and thinly sliced	raw
quince	4, peeled, cored, and quartered	raw
yellow mustard seeds	1 cup (145 g)	raw

Pickling couldn't be easier. I follow these basic techniques:

■ Use a one-to-one ratio of liquid to solids.

■ Blanch any hard vegetables or fruit, such as root vegetables, until just tender. Then, shock them in ice water and drain well before covering with hot pickling liquid.

■ Cut the vegetables for more intense pickling. The smaller the pieces, the more pickled they'll get.

CHAPTER 8

DESSERTS

CINNAMON-SUGAR "DOUGHNUTS"

SONHOS

Sonhos translates as "dreams," and that's how ethereal these are. Straight out of the fryer, these crisp puffs are light as air. At Aldea, we always serve them with sauces for dipping—the perennial classic caramel, then seasonal specialties ranging from rhubarb sauce to lemon curd. But they're also delicious alone with their cinnamon-sugar coating.

SERVES 8

sugar	¼ cup plus ¼ teaspoon (55 g)
unsalted butter	½ teaspoon
all-purpose flour	1 cup (150 g)
eggs	4 large
ground cinnamon	1 tablespoon
canola oil	as needed
Salted Caramel Sauce (page 205)	for serving
Concord Grape Jam (page 208)	for serving
Chocolate-Hazelnut Sauce (page 209)	for serving

In a medium saucepan, bring 1 cup (240 ml) water, ¼ teaspoon of the sugar, and the butter to a boil over high heat. Add the flour and stir continuously and vigorously until the mixture forms a ball. Reduce the heat to medium. Continue cooking, stirring vigorously, until the dough starts to puff and a thin layer of dough sticks to the bottom of the pan. The dough will be very stiff; just keep working it. Transfer it to a stand mixer fitted with the paddle attachment.

Beat on medium-low speed just to break up the ball. Add the eggs, one at a time, beating until smooth after each addition. Raise the speed to high and beat, scraping the bowl occasionally, until the eggs are fully incorporated and there are no clumps, about 1 minute. Don't overbeat the dough; the bowl should still be warm.

Transfer the dough to a container, let cool slightly, and refrigerate until chilled.

When you're ready to serve, combine the cinnamon and remaining ¼ cup (50 g) sugar in a medium bowl. Fill a medium saucepan with oil to a depth of 3 inches (7.5 cm). Heat to 300°F (150°C). Using a teaspoon cookie scoop or measuring teaspoon, carefully drop a few balls of dough into the hot oil. Don't crowd the pan. Adjust the heat to maintain the temperature. Cook until the sonhos float, puff, and are golden and cooked through, about 8 minutes. Immediately transfer to the cinnamon-sugar and gently toss to coat. Repeat with the remaining dough. Serve the sonhos hot with the sauces.

SALTED CARAMEL SAUCE

On one of our restaurant feedback cards, a woman wrote, "I love this sauce so much, I want to bathe in it." Weird, but I get what she's saying. It's that good.

MAKES ABOUT 2 CUPS (480 ML)

sugar	1¼ cups (250 g)
glucose (optional)	1 tablespoon
heavy cream	¾ cup (180 ml)
kosher salt	1 tablespoon
unsalted butter	2 tablespoons, cut in pieces, softened

In a medium saucepan, combine the sugar, 5 tablespoons (75 ml) water, and the glucose, if using.

Bring to a boil over medium heat, swirling the pan occasionally, until the mixture is amber. Reduce the heat to low and carefully and slowly whisk in the cream. The mixture will bubble up. Continue whisking until well combined. Whisk in the salt. Remove from the heat and transfer to a bowl. When lukewarm, stir in the butter, a little at a time, until well combined. Serve the caramel at room temperature. The caramel can be refrigerated in an airtight container for up to 1 week. Bring to room temperature before serving.

CINNAMON-SUGAR "DOUGHNUTS"

CONCORD GRAPE JAM

Intensely sweet-tart and a little musky, deep purple Concord grapes make the best homemade jam—worlds apart from the jarred stuff. I use this both in desserts, such as sonhos (page 204), and savory dishes, like my Foie Gras Terrine (page 124).

MAKES ABOUT 2 CUPS (640 G)

SPECIAL EQUIPMENT:
> FOOD MILL

Concord grapes 1 pound (455 g)
sugar 1½ cups (300 g)
limes 3

In a medium saucepan, combine the grapes and sugar. Zest the limes into the mixture. From the limes, squeeze ½ cup (120 ml) juice. Stir into the mixture. Cook over medium-low heat until thickened. The jam is ready when a dollop on a cold spoon holds its shape and doesn't run. Remove from the heat and pass through a food mill to remove the skins and seeds. Let cool to room temperature. The jam can be refrigerated in an airtight container for up to 2 weeks. Bring to room temperature before serving.

CHOCOLATE-HAZELNUT SAUCE

Be sure to start with high-quality chocolate for this silky sauce. I always use Valrhona.

MAKES ABOUT 2 CUPS (480 ML)

bittersweet chocolate (66% cacao)	4 ounces (115 g)
semisweet chocolate (40% cacao)	5½ ounces (155 g)
whole milk	1⅔ cups (405 ml)
nonfat dry milk	½ cup (60 g)
honey	2 tablespoons
kosher salt	pinch
whole blanched almonds	⅓ cup (50 g), toasted
whole peeled hazelnuts	1¼ cups (170 g), toasted

Combine the chocolates in a medium heatproof bowl. Fill a medium saucepan with water to a depth of 1 inch (2.5 cm) and bring to a simmer. Set the bowl of chocolate over the saucepan and melt, stirring occasionally.

Meanwhile, in a medium saucepan, combine the whole milk, dry milk, honey, and salt. Bring to a boil over medium heat.

In a food processor, pulse the almonds and hazelnuts until pasty. With the machine running, add the hot melted chocolate and blend well, then add the hot milk mixture in a slow, steady stream. Blend until well mixed. Press through a fine-mesh sieve. Serve warm or at room temperature. The sauce can be refrigerated in an airtight container for up to 1 week. Bring to room temperature before serving.

PUMPKIN FRITTERS

FILHOZES

Every Christmas, my mom and my aunts would stand over the stove frying these traditional doughnuts and I'd be right there too, ready to eat them hot out of the oil. They're actually good at room temperature as well and, honestly, at any time of year.

MAKES ABOUT 2 DOZEN

canola oil	for frying
ground cinnamon	1 tablespoon
sugar	6 tablespoons (75 g)
all-purpose flour	⅔ cup (85 g)
baking powder	¾ teaspoon
kosher salt	⅛ teaspoon
pureed pumpkin or squash (see Note)	⅔ cup (165 g)
egg	1 large

Fill a heavy, deep saucepan with oil to a depth of 2 inches (5 cm). Heat it to 300°F (150°C) and adjust the heat to maintain the temperature. In a medium bowl, stir together the cinnamon and 4 tablespoons (50 g) of the sugar and reserve.

Meanwhile, in another medium bowl, whisk together the flour, baking powder, and salt. In a large bowl, whisk together the pumpkin, egg, and remaining 2 tablespoons sugar until smooth. Sprinkle the flour mixture over the pumpkin and whisk until just combined.

Working in batches, carefully drop mounded teaspoons of the dough into the hot oil, spacing them apart. Don't crowd the pan and adjust the heat to maintain the oil temperature. After about 30 seconds, the dough balls should rise to the surface. Cook, turning occasionally, until golden brown and cooked through, about 10 minutes. You can open one to make sure there's no raw dough in the center.

Drain on paper towels and roll in the cinnamon-sugar. Repeat with the remaining dough and serve the fritters hot or warm.

NOTE *You can use the roasted butternut squash and sugar pumpkin flesh from the Roasted Squash Soup (page 157) here: Simply puree the roasted squash and pumpkin without any added liquid. Other pureed, steamed, or cooked squash may be too wet for the batter. If you don't have time to roast and puree squash, use canned packed pumpkin instead.*

DESSERT

My Lisbon friends first introduced me to Pastéis de Belém during the World's Fair. Founded in 1837, this pastry shop specializes in the egg custard tarts originally created in the nearby monastery. The tarts are now a national treasure and are served around the world in Portuguese bakeries. At Belém, my friends and I would buy a box and we'd polish off a dozen at a time. I'm still tempted to when I'm at this landmark bakery. There's always a line out the door because these are easily the best pastéis de nata. (The recipe's safeguarded in a locked room.) The bakers blast them in blazing hot ovens until the sweet shells are as crackly as chips and the tops are blistered with dark caramelized spots. Plus, they serve them warm. I sprinkle cinnamon on mine before taking a bite; I love how the crunchy pastry gives way to the creamy, rich sweet egg custard.

As much as I love the composed, seasonally driven desserts we serve at Aldea, I'm often drawn to the home-style Portuguese sweets I grew up eating. A lot of the traditional rich desserts are tooth-achingly sweet, so I've adjusted the sugar to my taste. But I've kept the soul of the dishes—the creaminess of rice pudding, the airiness of freshly fried doughnuts, the crunch of buttery cookies. Even though I'm not a pastry chef, I really enjoy making dessert. There's something especially satisfying about creating the ending to the meal, to leaving diners with a bite that will make them as happy as a kid in a pastry shop.

CRISPY EGG CUSTARD TARTS

This is, hands down, my favorite Portuguese dessert. The key to making them at home is getting your oven as hot as you can. If it still isn't hot enough to caramelize the tops of the custards, run them under the broiler just before serving.

MAKES 4 DOZEN

PORTUGUESE PUFF PASTRY

unsalted butter	¾ cup (12 ounces/180 g), softened
all-purpose flour	1¾ cups (225 g), plus more for the work surface
salt	¼ teaspoon

FILLING

sugar	1 cup (200 g)
cinnamon stick	1
whole milk	1 cup plus 6 tablespoons (330 ml)
all-purpose flour	½ cup (75 g)
egg yolks	6 large
ground cinnamon	for serving

MAKE THE PASTRY: In a small bowl, whisk the butter until it is the consistency of sour cream.

In the bowl of an electric mixer fitted with the dough hook, combine the flour, salt, and ⅔ cup (165 ml) water. Mix on low speed until the mixture comes together and is tacky, scraping the bowl down occasionally.

Transfer to a well-floured work surface and form into a 1-inch- (2.5-cm-) thick rectangle. With a well-floured rolling pin, roll the dough into a ½-inch- (12-mm-) thick rectangle that's 10 inches (25 cm) long. Cover with plastic wrap and let rest for 15 minutes.

Remove the plastic wrap and roll the dough into a 15-inch (38-cm) square. Spread one third of the butter on the bottom half of the dough, leaving a 1-inch (2.5-cm) rim. Using a bench scraper, fold the top half of the dough over the butter. Press the edges to seal. Pat the dough with a rolling pin and rotate the dough so that the seam is facing you. Roll into a 15-inch (38-cm) square again. Spread half of the remaining butter on the bottom half of the dough, leaving a 1-inch (2.5-cm) rim. Using a bench scraper, fold the top half of the dough over the butter. Press the edges to seal. Pat the dough with a rolling pin and rotate the dough so that the seam is facing you. Now, roll into an 18-inch (46-cm) square.

Spread the remaining butter all over the dough, leaving a 1-inch (2.5-cm) rim. Starting with the edge closest to you, roll the dough into a log. Wrap in plastic wrap and refrigerate until very firm, at least 2 hours and preferably overnight.

MAKE THE FILLING: Preheat the oven to 500°F (260°C), on the convection setting if you have it.

In a medium saucepan, combine the sugar, cinnamon stick, and ⅔ cup (165 ml) water. Bring to a boil and boil for 1 minute. Let sit until you're ready to use it.

Roll the firm log of pastry on a lightly floured surface until 1 inch (2.5 cm) in diameter. Trim the ends, then cut the log into 48 (½-inch/12-mm) slices. Place each slice into the cavity of a mini muffin tin, with the cut side of the spiral facing up. Use your thumb to press the center of the spiral into the bottom of the pan and continue pressing to evenly flatten the dough against the bottom and sides of the cavity, extending about ¹⁄₁₆-inch (3 mm) above the rim of the pan. The dough should be about ¹⁄₁₆ inch (3 mm) thick, with the bottom a bit thicker than the sides. Repeat with the remaining dough. Refrigerate until firm, at least 10 minutes.

While the dough chills, finish the filling: In a small saucepan, heat 1 cup plus 1 tablespoon (255 ml) of the milk over medium-low heat until bubbles begin to form around the edges. In a large bowl, whisk the flour with the remaining 5 tablespoons (75 ml) milk. Continue whisking while adding the hot milk in a slow, steady stream. Discard the cinnamon stick

from the sugar syrup and whisk the syrup into the milk mixture in a steady stream. Return to the saucepan and cook over low heat, whisking constantly, until thickened.

Add the yolks to the mixture and whisk until well combined. Strain through a fine-mesh sieve, then pour the warm filling into the pastry shells until they're three-quarters full.

Bake until the shells are dark golden brown and crisp, the custards are set, and the tops are blackened in spots, about 20 minutes. Let cool in the pans on wire racks for 5 minutes, then transfer to wire racks. Sprinkle with cinnamon and serve warm.

CHOCOLATE SALAMI

When I was a kid, I always begged my mom for this treat. It's basically soft chocolate ganache rolled with buttery cookies and sliced to look like salami. In Portugal, store-bought Bolacha Maria cookies are used, but I prefer homemade Butter Cookies (opposite).

MAKES ABOUT 3 DOZEN

chopped bittersweet chocolate (66% cacao)	1½ cups (200 g)
unsalted butter	11 tablespoons (5½ ounces/150 g), softened
sugar	½ cup (100 g)
pasteurized egg yolks	3 large
dark rum	2 tablespoons
Butter Cookies (opposite)	3½ cups (300 g) ½-inch (12-mm) pieces
skinless hazelnuts (optional)	¾ cup (100 g), toasted

Melt the chocolate in the top of a double boiler or a heatproof bowl set over simmering water, stirring occasionally, until smooth. Remove from the heat.

In a large bowl, whisk the butter until it is the consistency of sour cream, then whisk in the sugar until it dissolves a little. Add the yolks and whisk until smooth. Whisk in the warm chocolate until smooth, then the rum. Fold in the cookies and hazelnuts, if using.

Refrigerate until a little firmer, about 30 minutes. Transfer to a large sheet of parchment paper, dolloping the mixture in an 18-inch- (46-cm-) long line. Roll into a 2-inch- (5-cm-) diameter log. Refrigerate until very firm, preferably overnight. When you're ready to serve, cut the log into ½-inch (12-mm) slices.

BUTTER COOKIES

This is the ultimate all-purpose cookie. Most Portuguese versions are too sweet and rich for me, so I cut back on the sugar. But I kept the generous dose of egg yolks.

MAKES ABOUT 50

all-purpose flour	1½ cups (225 g)
baking powder	1 teaspoon
salt	½ teaspoon
unsalted butter	¾ cup (12 ounces/170 g), softened
sugar	¾ cup (150 g)
egg yolks	4 large

Sift the flour, baking powder, and salt into a medium bowl.

In the bowl of a stand mixer fitted with the paddle attachment, beat the butter until soft. Add the sugar and beat on medium-high speed until smooth. On medium speed, beat in the egg yolks until well blended, scraping down the sides of the bowl. On low speed, beat in the dry ingredients until just combined.

Form the dough into two logs, each 2 inches (5 cm) in diameter, and wrap in plastic wrap. Refrigerate until firm.

To bake, preheat the oven to 300°F (150°C). Line baking sheets with parchment paper.

Cut the dough logs into ½-inch (12-mm) slices. Place on the baking sheets ½ inch (12 mm) apart. Bake until golden, about 12 minutes. Let cool completely on the sheets on wire racks. The cookies can be stored in an airtight container for up to 3 days.

CORN PUDDING

Corn works as a natural thickener in this Brazilian pudding that resembles a corn casserole. You can spoon out this silky, homey dessert straight from the dishes.

SERVES 6

corn	6 medium ears
heavy cream	1 cup (240 ml)
whole milk	½ cup (120 ml)
eggs	4 large
sugar	6 tablespoons (75 g)
unsalted butter	½ cup (4 ounces/112 g), softened
all-purpose flour	2 tablespoons
baking powder	2 teaspoons
kosher salt	1 teaspoon

Preheat the oven to 300°F (150°C).

Set a box grater over a bowl and grate the ears of corn into the bowl. You want 2 cups (330 g) of kernels with their milky juices. Transfer to a blender and add the remaining ingredients. Blend on medium-high speed until well mixed but still a little chunky. You should have about 6 cups (1.4 L). Divide the mixture among six (8-ounce/240-ml) shallow ramekins.

Bake until the tops are puffed and light golden brown and a thin knife inserted in the centers comes out clean, about 20 minutes. Serve the puddings hot, warm, or at room temperature.

CINNAMON-VANILLA RICE PUDDING

During my childhood, every family celebration ended with this classic rice pudding. My uncle Anibal was an expert at sprinkling cinnamon on top in precise patterns. It's totally old school. He also made the tastiest pudding, but he held his recipe tight. To this day, I don't know his formula. I've done my best to recreate his killer version here.

SERVES 4

sugar	6 tablespoons (75 g)
vanilla bean	1 whole, split and seeds scraped
whole milk	3¾ cups (900 ml), plus more as needed
Carolina rice	⅔ cup (140 g)
kosher salt	½ teaspoon
cinnamon sticks	2
Vinho Verde–Poached Plums (page 218)	for serving

In a large saucepan, combine the sugar and vanilla seeds. Use your fingers to rub the seeds into the sugar to distribute evenly. Add the vanilla pod, milk, rice, salt, and cinnamon and stir well.

Bring to a simmer over medium-low heat, stirring occasionally. Adjust the heat to maintain a low simmer and cook, stirring and scraping the bottom of the pan occasionally, until the liquid is mostly absorbed and the rice is tender but still chewy, about 45 minutes.

If the mixture is too thick, add a little milk to thin it. Remove the vanilla pod and cinnamon sticks and serve the pudding hot, warm, room temperature, or cold with the plums.

VINHO VERDE-POACHED PLUMS

Any stone fruit aside from prune plums (also known as sugar plums) works well here. A quick poach in simple syrup is a nice way for stone fruits to pick up the flavor of spices. You can use the poaching liquid three times. After that, stir it into a cocktail, make homemade soda, or set it with gelatin into a gelée. The fruit here goes well on Cinnamon-Vanilla Rice Pudding (page 217), but it's also great with warm Olive Oil Cake (page 221), vanilla ice cream, panna cotta, sour cream, or crème fraîche.

SERVES 4

orange	1 medium
dry white vinho verde	⅔ cup (165 ml)
peach liqueur	⅔ cup (165 ml)
sugar	¾ cup (150 g)
cinnamon sticks	2
whole cloves	3, lightly crushed
whole star anise	2
plums	4 large, cut into ½-inch (12-mm) wedges

Use a vegetable peeler to remove the orange zest in strips. Transfer to a medium saucepan and add the vinho verde, liqueur, sugar, cinnamon, cloves, star anise, and ½ cup (120 ml) water. Bring to a simmer over medium-low heat, stirring to dissolve the sugar. Remove from the heat and let sit for 10 minutes.

Strain the syrup through a fine-mesh sieve and return to the saucepan. Add the plums; they should be immersed in the syrup in a single layer. Very gently simmer over medium-low heat, turning the pieces occasionally, just until the fruit becomes translucent, about 7 minutes. Remove from the heat and let sit for 10 minutes. Use the plums immediately, removing the fruit from the syrup with a slotted spoon. Reserve the syrup in the refrigerator to use again.

STRAWBERRIES WITH RICOTTA CREAM

Even when it comes to sweets, I'm inspired by the seasons. This dessert was driven by the gorgeous Tri-Star strawberries available only from late spring to late summer at the Union Square Greenmarket. I wanted a simple cream to highlight their natural sweetness.

SERVES 4

heavy cream	¾ cup (180 ml)
whole green cardamom pods	5, lightly crushed
egg yolks	2 large
sugar	2 tablespoons, plus more to taste
whole-milk ricotta cheese (see Note)	¾ cup (165 g)
strawberries	2 cups (300 g) small or quartered large
roasted pistachios	chopped, for serving

In a medium saucepan, combine the cream and cardamom. Bring to a simmer over medium heat, then remove from the heat, cover, and let steep for 30 minutes. Pick out and discard the cardamom. Bring the cream back to a simmer over medium heat.

In a medium bowl, whisk the egg yolks and sugar together until well combined. Continue whisking while adding the simmering cream in a slow, steady stream. Return the mixture to the saucepan and whisk over low heat until thickened, with fine bubbles (a candy thermometer should register 85°F/30°C). Remove from the heat, then whisk in the ricotta until smooth. Refrigerate or set the pan in a large bowl filled with ice and water until the ricotta cream is cold.

While the ricotta cream chills, prepare the strawberries. In a medium saucepan, toss the strawberries with sugar to taste and a splash of water. Heat over medium heat until just warm, about 2 minutes. Remove from the heat and let stand until cooled to room temperature. Serve the strawberries with the chilled cream and sprinkle with the pistachios.

NOTE *Use a really smooth, thick fresh ricotta here. If you can't find that and are using one that has a lumpy texture similar to cottage cheese, then strain it through a fine-mesh sieve first to remove the excess liquid. Once it's strained, puree it in a blender or food processor until smooth.*

OLIVE OIL CAKE

A high-quality olive oil keeps this cake moist and adds another dimension of fruity flavor. Even though I usually plate this dessert with Strawberries with Ricotta Cream (page 219), strawberry sorbet, and Port Caramel (page 222), it also tastes great on its own.

MAKES ONE 13-BY-9-INCH
(33-BY-23-CM) CAKE

nonstick cooking spray	as needed
fruity olive oil, such as Arbequina	1 cup (240 ml)
whole milk	1 cup (240 ml)
eggs	3 large, at room temperature
freshly grated lemon zest	2 tablespoons
sugar	1⅔ cups (355 g)
all-purpose flour	2½ cups (385 g)
kosher salt	1½ teaspoons
baking powder	1 teaspoon
baking soda	½ teaspoon

Preheat the oven to 300°F (150°C). Lightly coat a 13-by-9-inch (33-by-23-cm) cake pan with nonstick cooking spray. Line the bottom of the pan with parchment paper and spray again.

In a medium bowl, whisk together the oil, milk, and eggs until smooth.

In a large bowl, rub the zest into the sugar with your fingertips. Whisk in the flour, salt, baking powder, and baking soda. Continue whisking while adding the wet ingredients in a slow, steady stream. Whisk just until smooth and well combined, then pour into the prepared pan.

Bake, rotating the pan halfway through, until the top is golden brown and springs back when gently pressed with your fingertip, about 30 minutes.

Let cool completely in the pan on a wire rack. Cut into pieces to serve. The cake can be stored in an airtight container overnight.

PORT CARAMEL

Portugal's world-renowned fortified wine makes for an intense caramel sauce. This is delicious on everything from ice cream to cakes to fruit.

MAKES ABOUT 3 CUPS (720 ML)

sugar 1¼ cups (266 g)
ruby port 1⅔ cups (405 ml)

In a large saucepan, combine the sugar and 1 cup (240 ml) water. Bring to a boil over medium heat, stirring to dissolve the sugar. Cook, swirling the pan occasionally, until dark amber, about 13 minutes.

Very slowly and carefully stir in the port; the mixture will bubble up. Be sure to add the port in a slow, steady stream. If you add it too quickly, it can cause the sugar to seize.

Reduce the heat to medium-low and cook until reduced significantly, about 15 minutes. Drop a little on a cold plate; the mixture shouldn't run. Transfer to a bowl and let cool to room temperature. This sauce can be refrigerated in an airtight container for up to 1 month. Bring to room temperature before serving.

PORTS AND MADEIRAS

At the end of nearly every casual meal in Portugal, the server will set down small dessert-wine glasses and pour aguardente, their version of homemade moonshine. Classier joints offer our national fortified wines: port and madeira. You really can't go wrong with any of the choices. Just choose what you like:

Port, from Douro Valley's sun-drenched city of Porto, falls into three main categories: white, ruby, and tawny. The first is made from white grapes and is pale white to amber. Even seco (dry) varieties are pretty sweet, so you can imagine how sugary doce (sweet) varieties are. Given that profile, these are often served as aperitifs or mixed with cocktails. Ruby ports are slightly less sweet and the longer they age, the more complex and less tannic they are. They're ideal for pairing with cheese and chocolate at the end of the meal, but are sometimes offered as an aperitif too. The best of the three is tawny port. Ranging from amber to deep brown, tawnies are slow-aged in wood, giving them complex fruit and nut notes. They're great chilled as an aperitif or digestive, either alone or with cheese.

Madeira, both white and red, is almost exclusively served at the end of the meal and can range from tooth-achingly sweet to off-dry, which you can determine by the grape variety. Going from dry to sweet: Sercial, Terrantez, Verdelho, Boal, and Malvasia. They all have a distinctive nutty-caramel flavor from aging in wood and are a great way to finish a meal.

CHAPTER 9

BUILDING BLOCKS: STOCKS, SAUCES, OILS, AND SEASONINGS

CHICKEN STOCK

MAKES ABOUT 4 QUARTS (3.8 L)

chicken bones	8 pounds (3.6 kg), cut into 1-inch (2.5-cm) pieces
white onion	1 medium, chopped
carrots	2 medium, peeled and chopped
celery stalks	2 medium, chopped
garlic	1 head, cut in half crosswise
whole white peppercorns	1 teaspoon, cracked
fresh bay leaf	1, notches torn every ½ inch (12 mm)
fresh parsley	4 sprigs
fresh thyme	1 sprig

In a very large, wide stockpot, cover the chicken bones with cold water. Bring to a boil over high heat and then drain. Return the bones to the pot.

Add the onion, carrots, celery, garlic, peppercorns, bay leaf, parsley, and 4 quarts (3.8 L) cold water (or enough to cover the solids). Bring to a slow bubble, reduce the heat to maintain a simmer, and simmer for 3 hours, skimming any foam that rises to the surface.

Remove from the heat and add the thyme. Let cool slightly, then strain through a fine-mesh sieve. Discard the solids. Use the stock immediately, refrigerate for up to 2 days, or freeze for up to 2 months.

VARIATION

VEGETABLE STOCK Omit the chicken bones and quadruple the vegetable quantities. Proceed as above, cooking the vegetables in oil until tender before adding the water.

BROWN
CHICKEN STOCK

MAKES ABOUT 2 QUARTS (2 L)

chicken	1 whole (4 pounds/1.8 kg)
extra-virgin olive oil	as needed
unsalted butter	3 tablespoons
shallot	1, sliced
garlic cloves	2
coriander seeds	1 teaspoon
whole white peppercorns	1 teaspoon
Chicken Stock (opposite)	3 quarts (2.8 L)

Preheat the oven to 500°F (260°C), on the convection setting if you have it.

Cut the wishbone out of the chicken and reserve. Cut the chicken into 8 pieces: 2 breast halves, 2 thighs, 2 drumsticks, and 2 wings. Separate the wings from the drumettes and tips and cut each piece in half. Cut the back bones into 2-inch (5-cm) pieces.

Heat a large, deep, oven-safe sauté pan over high heat until really hot. Coat with oil and add the backbones, wing pieces, wishbone, and neck in a single layer. (Reserve the meaty parts for another recipe.) Be careful; the oil will pop and the meat will smoke. Add 2 tablespoons of the butter and cook until the chicken starts to caramelize on the bottom of the pan, about 5 minutes. Scrape the browned bits from the bottom and stir well. Cook for about 5 minutes more, then transfer the pan to the oven.

Roast the chicken bones for 10 minutes, then very carefully drain off about half of the fat from the pan so that the bottom has just a thin layer of fat. Return the pan to the stove and set over medium-high heat.

Add the remaining 1 tablespoon butter, the shallot, garlic, coriander, and peppercorns. Cook, stirring and scraping the pan, until the aromatics are tender and the spices fragrant. Add 1½ quarts (1.4 L) of the stock, bring to a boil, and boil hard until reduced to a thick, dark brown glaze (about 2 cups/480 ml).

Add the remaining 1½ quarts (1.4 L) stock and simmer just until reduced to 2 quarts (2 L). Press the stock through a fine-mesh sieve. Discard the solids. Use the stock immediately, refrigerate for up to 2 days, or freeze for up to 2 months.

PORK STOCK

MAKES ABOUT 2 QUARTS (2 L)

canola oil	2 tablespoons
pork shoulder bones	2 pounds (910 g)
kosher salt	as needed
white onion	1 cup chopped (120 g)
celery stalk	½ cup sliced (50 g)
carrot	½ cup peeled and sliced (65 g)
garlic	½ head
tomato paste	1 tablespoon

Preheat the oven to 400°F (205°C) with a roasting pan inside.

Coat the hot pan with the oil and add the bones, turning to coat with the oil. Season with salt. Roast until golden brown, 20 to 30 minutes.

Add the onion, celery, carrot, and garlic. Roast, stirring occasionally, for 10 minutes, then stir again and cook for 15 minutes more. Stir in the tomato paste and roast for 2 minutes. Transfer the mixture to a 4-quart (3.8-L) saucepan. Deglaze the roasting pan with 1 cup (240 ml) water, stirring and scraping up the browned bits. Pour the water into the saucepan. Add more water to the saucepan to cover the solids by 2 inches (5 cm).

Bring to a simmer, then adjust the heat to maintain a slow bubble, uncovered, for 3 hours. Skim the scum that rises to the surface and discard. Press the stock through a fine-mesh sieve. Discard the solids. Use the stock immediately, refrigerate for up to 2 days, or freeze for up to 2 months.

VARIATIONS

BEEF STOCK Substitute beef bones for the pork bones; proceed as above.

LAMB STOCK Substitute lamb bones for the pork bones; proceed as above.

PORK JUS

MAKES ABOUT 1 CUP (240 ML)

extra-virgin olive oil	2 tablespoons
pork shoulder **or other stew meat**	2 pounds (910 g), cut into 1-inch (2.5-cm) chunks
kosher salt	as needed
white onion	½, cut into 1-inch (2.5-cm) slices
celery stalk	1, cut into ½-inch (2.5-cm) slices
carrot	½, peeled and cut into ½-inch (2.5-cm) slices
garlic cloves	3, crushed
tomato paste	1 tablespoon
Pork Stock (page 228)	1 recipe, as needed

Preheat the oven to 400°F (205°C) with a roasting pan inside.

Coat the hot pan with the oil and add the pork, turning to coat with the oil. Season with salt. Roast until golden brown, 20 to 30 minutes. Add the onion, celery, carrot, and garlic. Roast, stirring occasionally, until golden brown, about 15 minutes. Stir in the tomato paste and roast for 1 more minute. Transfer the mixture to a rondeau (wide, shallow pot).

Add just enough stock to cover the solids. Bring to a boil, then simmer and reduce the stock until the solids are glazed. Repeat the process three times, adding just enough stock to cover the solids each time. (This process results in a deeper, more flavorful jus.)

Finally, add enough stock to cover the solids by 1 inch (2.5 cm), bring to a boil, then reduce the heat to maintain a slow simmer. Simmer for 2 hours, then press through a fine-mesh sieve. Discard the solids. Transfer the jus to a clean rondeau, bring to a simmer, and reduce to 1 cup, until thick enough to coat the back of a spoon. Use the jus immediately, refrigerate for up to 2 days, or freeze for up to 2 months.

VARIATIONS

BEEF JUS Substitute a stew cut of beef for the pork; proceed as above.

LAMB JUS Substitute a stew cut of lamb for the pork; proceed as above.

CORIANDER DASHI

This variation on a classic Japanese stock includes a fresh note from cilantro. The kombu and bonito flakes can be found in Asian markets or online.

MAKES ABOUT 1 QUART (960 ML)

coriander seeds	2 tablespoons
kombu	1 (12-by-5-inch/30.5-by-12-cm) sheet, halved
bonito flakes	½ cup packed (7 g)
fresh cilantro	¼ cup packed (20 g)
soy sauce	2 tablespoons
fresh lemon juice	1 tablespoon
kosher salt and freshly ground white pepper	to taste

In a large saucepot, heat the coriander over medium heat, tossing occasionally, until toasted and fragrant. Add 1 quart (960 ml) water and the kombu. Bring to a simmer, then adjust the heat so that the liquid lightly steams for 45 minutes. Bubbles shouldn't break the surface.

Discard the kombu and bring the liquid to a gentle simmer. Stir in the bonito and cilantro and remove from the heat. Let stand for 15 minutes. Strain through a cheesecloth-lined fine-mesh sieve. Stir in the soy sauce and lemon juice. Season with salt and pepper, adding just enough so that the ocean flavors come through. Use the dashi immediately, refrigerate for up to 2 days, or freeze for up to 2 months.

SHRIMP ESSENCE

MAKES ABOUT 2 QUARTS (2 L)

SPECIAL EQUIPMENT:
> IMMERSION BLENDER
> FOOD MILL

canola oil	as needed
shrimp heads	2 pounds (910 g)
white onion	½, thinly sliced
fennel bulb	½, thinly sliced
celery stalks	2, thinly sliced
shallots	5, thinly sliced
garlic cloves	3, crushed
fennel seeds	1 tablespoon
whole star anise	1
saffron threads	1 tablespoon
brandy	½ cup (120 ml)
Pernod	½ cup (120 ml)
unsalted butter	1 teaspoon
tomato paste	1 teaspoon
fresh tarragon	2 sprigs
fresh parsley	2 sprigs
xanthan gum (see Note)	as needed

Heat a large, wide, deep saucepan over medium-high heat. Coat the bottom with a thin layer of oil. Add the shrimp heads and cook, stirring occasionally, until browned. Add the onion, fennel bulb, celery, shallots, garlic, fennel seeds, star anise, and saffron. Sweat, stirring occasionally, until the vegetables are soft but not browned. Deglaze with the brandy, stirring until the liquid has evaporated. Add the Pernod and cook until the liquid has evaporated. Stir in the butter and tomato paste and cook, stirring, for 2 minutes. Add 2 quarts (2 L) water to cover, heat to a simmer, and simmer for 30 minutes. Remove from the heat, add the tarragon and parsley, and let stand for 15 minutes.

Pass the mixture through a food mill, then press through a fine-mesh sieve. Weigh the strained mixture and calculate 0.2% of the total weight. That's the amount of xanthan gum you'll need. Cool the shrimp liquid, then stir in the xanthan gum. Puree with an immersion blender. Transfer to a saucepan and heat over medium heat until barely bubbling. Keep hot. Use the sauce immediately, refrigerate for up to 2 days, or freeze for up to 2 months.

VARIATIONS

SHRIMP STOCK Omit the fennel seeds, star anise, saffron, brandy, Pernod, and xanthan gum. Proceed as above.

LOBSTER STOCK Make the shrimp stock above, substituting the shells and head from 1 whole lobster for the shrimp heads.

NOTE *Xanthan gum, now available in supermarkets and also online, gives the sauce body.*

GOAN SPICE MIX

MAKES ABOUT ¼ CUP (40 G)

coriander seeds	2 tablespoons
cumin seeds	2 tablespoons
dried bird's eye chile	1, crumbled, or 1 teaspoon crushed red chile flakes
ground turmeric	½ teaspoon

In a small skillet, heat the coriander, cumin, and chile over medium heat, tossing occasionally, until toasted and fragrant. Remove from the heat and toss in the turmeric. Let cool completely, then grind in a spice grinder until powdery. The spice mix can be stored in an airtight container for up to 3 days.

REFOGADO

The Portuguese version of soffritto is integral to many traditional recipes. At Aldea, we make large amounts to use in a number of our dishes. If you plan to make many of the dishes in this book regularly, double, triple, or even quadruple the quantities here and keep a stash in the refrigerator. You want the flavors to stay fresh, though, so you should whip up a new batch every three days.

MAKES ABOUT ¼ CUP (60 ML)

extra-virgin olive oil	2 tablespoons
white onion	½ cup diced (60 g)
garlic cloves	3, chopped
saffron threads (optional)	pinch
tomato	1, peeled, seeded, and diced
pimentón (sweet smoked paprika)	1½ teaspoons
fresh bay leaf	1, notches torn every ½ inch (12 mm)

Heat a medium saucepan over medium-low heat. Coat with the oil, then add the onion and garlic. Sweat, stirring occasionally, until the onion is light golden brown. Add the saffron, if using, and cook, stirring, for 2 minutes. Add the tomato, raise the heat to medium, and cook, stirring occasionally, until the tomato releases its juices, then becomes dry. Stir in the pimentón and bay leaf.

Let the refogado cool, then refrigerate it in an airtight container for up to 3 days. Discard the bay leaf before using.

PIRI PIRI

Our national hot sauce is a must-have condiment for chile-heads. Even though jarred varieties are easy to find at stores, this homemade version can't be beat. It's especially tasty on hearty, rustic dishes.

MAKES ABOUT ¾ CUP (180 ML)

extra-virgin olive oil	as needed
yellow onion	¾ cup finely diced (90 g)
garlic cloves	3, minced
fresh bay leaf	1, notches torn every ½ inch (12 mm)
kosher salt	to taste
dried red piri piri peppers or bird's eye chiles (see Note)	½ cup (20 g)
red bell pepper	½ cup minced (75 g)
fresh red piri piri pepper or bird's eye chile	½, seeded and minced
bourbon	2 tablespoons
pimentón (smoked sweet paprika)	1 teaspoon
sherry vinegar	2 tablespoons

Heat a small saucepan over medium-low heat. Add enough oil to coat the bottom, then add the onion, garlic, bay leaf, and a pinch of salt. Cook, stirring occasionally, until the onion is golden and tender, about 7 minutes.

Add the dried chiles to the pan with enough oil to cover them. Bring to a boil, then reduce the heat to simmer gently until the dried chiles are softened, about 5 minutes. Stir in the bell pepper and fresh chile and simmer until tender, about 5 minutes.

Stir in the bourbon and pimentón and bring to a boil. Boil hard, stirring occasionally, for 3 minutes. Stir in the vinegar and remove from the heat.

Discard the bay leaf. Transfer to a blender or food processor and puree to the desired consistency. I prefer my piri piri smooth, but you can also make it more rustic and chunky if you like. Season to taste with salt. Cover and refrigerate for up to 1 month.

NOTE *I love the heat and fragrance of hot Portuguese piri piri chiles, but they're hard to find here. The closest approximation is dried or fresh Thai bird's eye chiles. You can experiment with different chiles, but make sure you choose hot ones.*

SQUID INK SAUCE

This sauce was inspired by my time staging with chef Martin Berasategui in Spain and brings a rich depth to my cuttlefish curry (page 67).

MAKES ABOUT ½ CUP (120 ML)

fenugreek seeds	1 teaspoon
fennel seeds	1 teaspoon
coriander seeds	1 teaspoon
whole star anise	1
extra-virgin olive oil	as needed
squid or cuttlefish trimmings	1 pound (455 g), rinsed and patted dry
white onion	1 small, thinly sliced
garlic cloves	3, crushed
fennel bulb	½ small, thinly sliced
carrot	½ small, peeled and thinly sliced
kosher salt	to taste
tomato paste	1 tablespoon
dry white vinho verde	½ cup (120 ml)
Chicken Stock (page 226)	¾ cup, or as needed
fresh tarragon	2 sprigs
squid ink	1 to 2 tablespoons

In a small skillet, heat the fenugreek, fennel seeds, coriander, and star anise over medium heat, tossing occasionally, until toasted and fragrant. Transfer to cheesecloth, then tie securely with kitchen twine.

Heat a large saucepan over medium-high heat. Add enough oil to coat the bottom of the pan, then add the squid or cuttlefish trimmings. Cook, stirring occasionally, until lightly caramelized.

Reduce the heat to medium-low and add the onion, garlic, fennel bulb, carrot, and a generous pinch of salt. Cook, stirring occasionally, until the vegetables are tender and golden, about 10 minutes. Add the tomato paste and cook, stirring, for 1 minute.

Add the vinho verde and cook, stirring occasionally, until the liquid has evaporated. Add the spice sachet and enough stock to cover the solids. Bring to a boil, then reduce the heat to simmer for 30 minutes. Add the tarragon, remove from the heat, and let steep for 15 minutes.

Strain through a fine-mesh sieve, pressing on the solids to extract as much liquid as possible. Discard the solids. Let the liquid cool completely, then stir in the squid ink to taste. Season with salt and use immediately.

HERB PUREE

MAKES ABOUT 2 CUPS (480 ML)

fresh parsley leaves	6 ounces (168 g)
fresh cilantro leaves	4 ounces (112 g)
fresh dill leaves	4 ounces (112 g)
extra-virgin olive oil	2 tablespoons
xanthan gum (optional; see Note, page 232)	pinch

Fill a large bowl with ice and water. Bring a large saucepan of water to a boil. Add all of the herbs and cook just until bright green, about 1 minute. Immediately transfer to the ice water. When cool, drain very well.

In a blender, combine the herbs, oil, xanthan gum (if using), and ½ cup (120 ml) water. Puree on high speed until very smooth. The puree can be refrigerated in an airtight container for up to 3 days.

PARSLEY OIL

MAKES ABOUT ½ CUP (120 ML)

kosher salt to taste
fresh parsley leaves 6 ounces (168 g)
canola oil ½ cup (120 ml)

Fill a medium bowl with ice and water. Bring a medium saucepan of water to a boil and salt lightly. Add the parsley leaves and cook until bright green, about 30 seconds. Immediately transfer to the ice water. When cool, drain well. Transfer to a clean kitchen towel, roll up, and wring dry. Repeat until the parsley is completely dry. Chop the dry parsley.

In a blender, combine the parsley and ¼ cup (60 ml) of the oil. Puree until smooth, then add the remaining ¼ cup (60 ml) oil in a steady stream with the machine running. Turn the blender to high and blend for 1 minute.

Set a large coffee filter over a container that holds it snugly and secure the edges of the filter to the container with a rubber band. Pour the oil into the filter and let it drip through. Discard the solids. The oil can be refrigerated in an airtight container for up to 3 days.

VARIATIONS

DILL OIL Substitute fresh dill leaves for the parsley. Proceed as above.

BASIL OIL Substitute fresh basil leaves for the parsley. Proceed as above.

GARLIC OIL

MAKES ABOUT ½ CUP (120 ML)

kosher salt to taste
garlic cloves 12, peeled
extra-virgin olive oil ½ cup (120 ml)

Fill a small bowl with ice and water. Bring a small saucepan of water to a boil and salt it lightly. Add the garlic and cook for **30** seconds. Immediately transfer to the ice water. When cool, drain well. Repeat this process two more times.

In a small saucepan, bring the oil and garlic to a simmer. Adjust the heat to maintain a gentle simmer until the garlic is tender, **20** to **30** minutes. Strain through a fine-mesh sieve; reserve the garlic cloves for another use. The oil can be refrigerated for up to **3** days.

APRICOT PUREE

MAKES ABOUT ½ CUP (120 ML)

dried California apricots ½ cup (65 g)
dry white vinho verde ¼ cup (60 ml)
sherry vinegar 1 tablespoon

In a medium saucepan, combine the apricots and vinho verde. Bring to a boil over medium heat and cook until the wine reduces by half. Stir in the vinegar. Transfer to a blender and puree until smooth. Press through a fine-mesh sieve. The puree can be refrigerated in an airtight container for up to 1 week.

TOMATO CONFIT

MAKES 2 DOZEN PIECES

beefsteak tomatoes	6, ripe but firm
garlic clove	1 large, shaved into paper-thin slices
fresh thyme	12 sprigs
kosher salt and freshly ground white pepper	to taste
extra-virgin olive oil	as needed

Preheat the oven to 250°F (120°C). Line a half sheet pan with parchment paper.

Fill a large bowl with ice and water. Bring a large saucepan of water to a boil. Slit an "x" in the base of each tomato and drop in the boiling water. Let sit for 10 seconds, then transfer to the ice water. Take the tomatoes out of the ice water, then peel, cut each into quarters, and seed.

Lay the tomato pieces skin-side down on the prepared pan and place 1 garlic shaving on top of each. Scatter the thyme sprigs over the tomatoes, season with salt and pepper, and drizzle with enough oil to very generously coat the tomatoes.

Bake until tender and starting to shrivel, about 4 hours. Discard the thyme and flip the tomatoes over to coat them in their cooking oil. Use immediately and reserve the oil for another use or refrigerate in an airtight container in the oil for up to 1 week.

PANTRY

You probably have almost
everything you need to cook with
Portuguese flavors. If you don't,
you'll be able to find most of it at
your local markets or online. That's
the great thing about this cuisine.
The seasonings are all familiar;
they're just put together in new,
flavorful ways. Here are the basics
you should keep on hand:

SALT AND PEPPER
Of course. I use Diamond Crystal kosher salt for cooking, fleur de sel and
Maldon flakes for finishing. Throughout, I call for freshly ground white
pepper because that's what we use at the restaurant to keep
our dishes looking pristine. Be sure to get fresh peppercorns; old ones
taste funky. Occasionally, I use black pepper too.

EXTRA-VIRGIN OLIVE OIL
For everything from cooking to finishing drizzles. I like fruity varieties
from Portugal and Spain, such as Arbequina.

HERBS
I use all the fresh herbs commonly used in Portugal, such as flat-leaf
parsley, cilantro, dill, mint, thyme, and oregano. When I'm at the Union
Square Greenmarket, I like to pick up specialty varieties, such as lemon
thyme. The one herb I use that's found throughout Portugal but is not
as common here is fresh bay leaf. Unlike dried dusty ones, these bring an
herbaceous, almost grassy, note to dishes. These glossy green leaves are
sold with all the other fresh herbs at the market.

PIMENTÓN (SMOKED SWEET PAPRIKA)
For a hit of smoky complexity. Paprika's often used in Portuguese
cuisine, but I like the Spanish smoked variety for an extra depth. A little
goes a long way.

DRY WHITE VINHO VERDE
The acidity and minerality of this Portuguese wine totally transforms
dishes. Look for the most recent varietals at the store. Given their great
value, keep a bottle on hand at all times and go ahead and have a glass
while you're at it.

SAUSAGES
Both chouriço and linguiça make their way into many Portuguese
dishes. These pork sausages are well spiced and taste best when cooked
gently. Look for them in well-stocked markets and keep them in the fridge.

PORTUGUESE OLIVE OILS

Even though olive oil has been produced in Portugal for centuries, the product has appeared in the international market only in the past few years. Traditionally, Portuguese producers would let the ripe olives fall from the trees and sit out for days or even weeks before pressing them. The slightly fermented olives made for robust, acidic oils with funk. Nowadays, producers from six regions (Norte Alentejo, Alentejo Interior, Moura, Ribatejo, Oporto, and Trás-os-Montes) are labeled Protected Designation of Origin (PDO). They're making refined oils that rival those from neighboring Mediterranean countries. Unique to the central and southern regions are Galega olives, which make exceptionally mellow and smooth oils. Generally, northern oils are more intense and southern ones fruitier. I especially like the balance of acidity, fruitiness, and peppery notes in PDO Moura oils.

Oils range in their tastes and textures, so it's best to sample the oil straight or with bread before deciding how to use it. If it tastes exceptional straight up, save it for drizzling and avoid cooking with it. I always go for fruit-forward oils and then decide how to use them depending on their other characteristics. Generally, here's what I do:

- mellow, delicate: perfect for raw fish because they won't overpower
- peppery, slightly acidic: great for shellfish with character, such as mussels or octopus
- piquant, rustic: ideal for meat

ACKNOWLEDGMENTS

FROM GEORGE AND GENEVIEVE:
We are so grateful for all the talented people who have made this book possible. At Stewart, Tabori, & Chang, our thanks go to our editors Natalie Kaire, Leslie Stoker, and Holly Dolce, art director John Gall, managing editor Sally Knapp, editorial assistant Sarah Massey, design manager Sebit Min, Claire Bamundo and Erin Hotchkiss in publicity and marketing, and copy editor and proofreaders Ann Martin Rolke, Holly Jennings, Elizabeth Norment, and Lisa Andruscavage. Thank you to our agents, Melissa Sarver, Elizabeth Kaplan, and Angela Miller.

Photographer Romulo Yanes and photo assistant Critter Knutsen captured the spirit of Aldea's food and kitchen. We appreciate their stunning shots, as well as their experience, flexibility, and good humor. Designer William van Roden translated the modern, rustic soul of Aldea into these pages with his creativity and sharp eye.

Our first-hand experiences in Portugal wouldn't have been possible without the expertise and generosity of our many hosts. Thank you to: Rui Abecassis, Pedro Veloso, and Mario Neves for your insider restaurant recommendations; Pedro Goncalves for fantastic meals; Sofia Alves for your photography; Blanche Orbe, Antonio Roquette, Miguel Vaz, and Pedro Lopes Vieira for a great time at the Esporão Winery and in the Alentejo; Nuno Antunes and Jorge Cosme for the beautiful and perfectly-located accommodations at the Bairro Alto Hotel in Lisbon; Gonçalo Narciso for the cool, chic rooms at the Bela Vista Hotel & Spa in Praia da Rocha; and Justin Ultee for the stunning seaside stay at the Vila Joya in Albufeira. A very special thanks to the extended Mendes family and everyone who so warmly welcomed us in the village of Ferreirós do Dão, especially Aunt Lourdes and cousins Louisa and John Carlo, Uncle Anibal and Aunt Alice, and Joao "Faia" Martina.

FROM GEORGE:
It's been five years since Aldea opened its doors. The restaurant—and this book—owe a debt of gratitude to: partners Adam Haber, Eddie Bernstein, Chris Courtiol, and Rob Walford; sous chefs Vicente Echeverria, Sarah Pliner, Aaron Silverman, and Tim Moody; pastry chefs Shelly Acuna, Johnny Iuzzini, and Miro Uskokovic; all of my cooks, both on the savory side and sweet; managers Heather Laiskonis, Heidi Young, Chris Lauber, and Mayara Nadel; servers Casey Courtney and Kim Souza; Juan "Juanito" Montes, Benigno Manzo, Miguel Rodriguez, Cesar Ramirez, and Ramon Julian; and my whole front-of-the-house team. A sincere thank you to my entire Aldea team throughout the years.

Before and after opening Aldea, I've learned so much from great mentors. I'm especially thankful for my professors at the Culinary Institute of America, Bill Keating, Edward Brown, David Bouley, Kurt Guttenbrunner, Alain Passard, Alain Ducasse, Martin Berasategui, Ferran Adrià, Marco Moreira, and Daniel Boulud.

Thank you to my friends and fellow chefs Mario Batali, Daniel Boulud, Erik Ripert, Daniel Patterson, and Sean Brock for championing this book with your thoughtful quotes.

This book came together through my collaboration with my writer, Genevieve. I appreciate her hard work and patience throughout the process.

Last but not least, my thanks go to my parents, sister, and extended family. They've influenced me deeply and set me on my path to becoming a chef. Obridago.

FROM GENEVIEVE:

Thank you to George for sharing your recipes, your time, and your stories to make this book possible. It's been an inspiring—and delicious—journey to see how you've returned to your roots in the kitchen.

I'm grateful to everyone at Aldea for welcoming me in the kitchen and dining room over the years. Thank you to the Mendes family, both in Connecticut and Portugal, for sharing your food and memories and for your hospitality and warmth.

As always, a big thank you to my family for your support and love.

ABOUT THE AUTHORS

George Mendes is the chef and owner of Aldea, his Portuguese-inspired restaurant, in New York City's Flatiron district, and a fast-rising national culinary star. He spent nearly twenty years honing his natural talent under the guidance of some of the world's greatest chefs before opening Aldea in May 2009. His restaurant won a star rating from the 2011, 2012, 2013, and 2014 Michelin Guides, along with glowing two-star reviews from both *New York* magazine and *The New York Times* and three-star reviews from *The Daily News*, *Bloomberg*, and *The New York Post*. In 2011, Mendes received one of the industry's most coveted honors when he was named one of *Food & Wine* magazine's ten "Best New Chefs."

Genevieve Ko is a New York City–based food writer and recipe developer. She has collaborated on books with chef Jean-Georges Vongerichten, including *Home Cooking with Jean-Georges*, and with celebrity chef Carla Hall, among others. In addition to her work on cookbooks, Genevieve has contributed to *Lucky Peach*, *Fine Cooking*, *Martha Stewart Living*, and other national magazines, and is contributing food editor of *Health*.

INDEX

Page numbers set in *italics* refer to photographs.

A

Abecassis, Rui, 29
Açorda (Tomato, Bread, and Egg Stew), 154, 155
Adrià, Ferran, 19–20
A Grade, 58–60, 59, 60
Agueda, 88–89
Albufeira, 145
Aldea, 12–13, 17, 20, 21, 32, 46
Alentejo, 116, 152, 154, 193, 245
Algarve, 145
almonds
    Green Beans with Peaches and Almonds, 168
    Sardines with Spring Greens and Almonds, 148, 149
Apple-Watercress Sauce, Seared Scallops with, 69
Apricot Puree, 242
Aromatic Black-Eyed Peas, 190
asparagus: Spring Pea Soup, 158

B

bacalhau. *See* salt cod
bacon
    Aromatic Black-Eyed Peas, 190
    Bacon-Braised Chickpeas, 191
    Brussels Sprouts with Quince and Bacon, 176, 177
    Cauliflower and Bacon Migas, 192, 193
    Eggs Baked with Peas, Linguiça, and Bacon, 100, 101
Barbot, Pascal, 184
Basil Oil, 239

beans
    Green Beans with Peaches and Almonds, 168
    See also black-eyed peas; chickpeas
beef
    Beef Jus, 230
    Beef Stock, 228
    Braised Oxtail, 132
beer, 32
beets
    Baby Goat with Beets, Cinnamon-Clove Yogurt, and Charred Bread Emulsion, 136, 137–38
    Smoked Baby Beets, 178
Benton hams, 99
Berasategui, Martin, 19, 237
black-eyed peas
    Aromatic Black-Eyed Peas, 190
    Octopus and Black-Eyed Pea Salad, 62, 63
blood sausage. *See* morcella
Bouley, David, 17
bread
    Baby Goat with Beets, Cinnamon-Clove Yogurt, and Charred Bread Emulsion, 136, 137–38
    Buttered Southern-Style Cornbread, 198, 199
    Roast Chicken Breasts with Bread Stuffing, 116
    Tomato, Bread, and Egg Stew (Açorda), 154, 155
    See also migas
broa, 199
Broccoli and Cauliflower, Coconut-Saffron, 171, 173
broccoli raab
    Broccoli Raab with Garlic and Red Chile Flakes, 175
    Salt Cod with Broccoli Raab, 34
Brown Chicken Stock, 227
Brown, Ed, 16

Brussels sprouts
    Brussels Sprouts with Quince and Bacon, 176, 177
    Wild Mushrooms with Brussels Sprouts, 180
Butter Cookies, 215
butternut squash: Roasted Squash Soup, 157

C

Cabbage and Tomato Soup, 156
Cake, Olive Oil, 220, 221
Caldeirada (Red Snapper with Shellfish, Tomato, and Saffron), 70–71, 72
Caldo Verde (Collard Greens Soup), 13, 153
Camoes, Luis de, 73
caramel
    Port Caramel, 222
    Salted Caramel Sauce, 205
carrots
    pickled, 200–201
    Sweet Carrot Custards, 179
Casa do Povo, 42–43
Casa Vidal, 88–89, 89
Cascais, 29
Casserole, Salt Cod, Potato, and Egg, 36, 37
cauliflower
    Cauliflower and Bacon Migas, 192, 193
    Coconut-Saffron Cauliflower and Broccoli, 171, 173
    pickled, 200–201
Cavaco Silva, Aníbal, 12, 47
Cervejaria da Esquina, 56, 187
Cervejaria Ramiro, 13, 50, 51, 99
chanterelles
    Fried Eggs with Chanterelles, Morcella, and Potatoes, 104, 105
    Shiitakes and Girolles with Wheat Berries, 184–85
    Wild Mushrooms with Brussels Sprouts, 180

Charred Bread Emulsion, Baby Goat with
Beets, Cinnamon-Clove Yogurt, and, *136*,
137–38
chicken
Chicken and Orzo Soup, 117–18, *119*
Roast Chicken Breasts with Bread Stuffing,
116
Spring Chicken Rice, 114–15
chicken stock
Brown Chicken Stock, 227
Chicken Stock, 226
Quick-Fix Stock, 115
chickpeas
Bacon-Braised Chickpeas, 191
Salt Cod and Chickpea Salad, *38*, 39
chocolate
Chocolate-Hazelnut Sauce, 209
Chocolate Salami, 214
chouriço. *See* sausage
cilantro
Clams Steamed with Vinho Verde, Garlic,
and Cilantro, 64, *65*
Coriander Dashi, 231
Herb Puree, 238
Cinnamon-Clove Yogurt, Baby Goat with
Beets, Charred Bread Emulsion, and, *136*,
137–38
Cinnamon-Sugar "Doughnuts" (Sonhos),
204, *207*
Cinnamon-Vanilla Rice Pudding, 217
clams, 50
Clams Steamed with Vinho Verde, Garlic,
and Cilantro, 64, *65*
Pork Belly and Clams with Pickles, 82–83,
85
Seafood Rice, 56, *57*
coconut
Coconut-Saffron Cauliflower and Broccoli,
171, *173*
Goan Cuttlefish Coconut Curry, *66*,
67–68
Goan Eggplant Curry, 170
Mussel Soup, 159–60, *161*
Zucchini and Squash with Coconut Sauce,
169
cod. *See* salt cod
Collard Greens Soup (Caldo Verde), *13*, 153
Concord Grape Jam, 208
Foie Gras Terrine with Concord Grape Jam
and Charred Quince, 124–25, *127*
confit
duck confit, 108–9
Octopus Confit, 61
Potatoes Confit, 195
Salt Cod Confit with Coriander Dashi,
Shiitake, and Litchi, 41
Tomato Confit, 243
cookies: Butter Cookies, 215

Coriander Dashi, 231
Salt Cod Confit with Coriander Dashi,
Shiitake, and Litchi, 41
Cornbread, Southern-Style, Buttered, *198*,
199
Corn Pudding, 216
crab: Red Snapper with Shellfish, Tomato, and
Saffron (Caldeirada), 70–71, *72*
cracklins
Duck Skin Cracklins, 112
Spiced Pork Belly Cracklins, 98
Croquettes, Salt Cod and Potato, *25*, 28
cucumbers
Iceberg, Cucumber, and Tomato Salad, 144
pickled, 200–201
Tuna with Cucumber, Smoked Paprika, and
Vinho Verde, 76, *77*
Cumin Yogurt, Crispy Pigs' Ears with Ramps
and, 94, *95*
Cured Pork Loin, 87
curry
Goan Cuttlefish Coconut Curry, *66*,
67–68
Goan Eggplant Curry, 170
custard
Crispy Egg Custard Tarts (Pastéis de Nata),
211, 212–13, *213*
Sweet Carrot Custards, 179
Cuttlefish Coconut Curry, Goan, *66*, 67–68

D

Dashi, Coriander, 231
Salt Cod Confit with Coriander Dashi,
Shiitake, and Litchi, 41
desserts, 202–22
about, 211
Butter Cookies, 215
Chocolate-Hazelnut Sauce, 209
Chocolate Salami, 214
Cinnamon-Sugar "Doughnuts" (Sonhos),
204, *207*
Cinnamon-Vanilla Rice Pudding, 217
Concord Grape Jam, 208
Corn Pudding, 216
Crispy Egg Custard Tarts (Pastéis de Nata),
211, 212–13, *213*
Olive Oil Cake, *220*, 221
Port Caramel, 222
Pumpkin Fritters (Filhozes), 210
Salted Caramel Sauce, 205
Strawberries with Ricotta Cream, 219
Vinho Verde-Poached Plums, 218
Dill Oil, 239
"Doughnuts," Cinnamon-Sugar, 204, *207*
Ducasse, Alain, 18–19
duck
Duck Rice, 108–10, *111*
Duck Skin Cracklins, 112
See also foie gras

E

Eggplant Curry, Goan, 170
eggs
Eggs Baked with Peas, Linguiça, and Bacon,
100, 101
Farm Egg, Salt Cod, Black Olives, and
Crunchy Potatoes, *30*, 31, *33*
Fried Eggs with Chanterelles, Morcella, and
Potatoes, *104*, 105
Linguiça, Chouriço, and Parsley Omelet,
102, *103*
Salt Cod, Potato, and Egg Casserole, 36,
37
Tomato, Bread, and Egg Stew (Açorda),
154, *155*
See also custard
El Bulli, 19–20
Escabeche, Partridge, 120
Esquina, 56, 187

F

fava beans, 152
Fava Beans with Morcella and Mint, 166,
167
Spring Chicken Rice, 114–15
Ferreirós do Dão, 12, 14, *42–43*, 99, 130, *131*
Filhozes (Pumpkin Fritters), 210
fish, 72–77
about, 73
Grilled Sardines with Charred Peppers,
74, *75*
Red Snapper with Shellfish, Tomato, and
Saffron (Caldeirada), 70–71, *72*
Sardines with Spring Greens and Almonds,
148, 149
Tuna, Tomato, and Onion Salad, 146, *147*
Tuna with Cucumber, Smoked Paprika, and
Vinho Verde, 76, *77*
See also salt cod
foie gras
Foie Gras Terrine with Concord Grape Jam
and Charred Quince, 124–25, *127*
Saffron Rice with Seared Shrimp and Foie
Gras, 54–55
Fritters, Pumpkin (Filhozes), 210

G

Gamba, Sandro, 18
game. *See* partridge; quail; venison
garlic
Broccoli Raab with Garlic and Red Chile
Flakes, 175
Clams Steamed with Vinho Verde, Garlic,
and Cilantro, 64, *65*
Garlic Oil, 241
Garlic Seared Shrimp, 46, 48, *49*

Girolles and Shiitakes with Wheat Berries, 184–85
Goan Cuttlefish Coconut Curry, 66, 67–68
Goan Eggplant Curry, 170
Goan Spice Mix, 233
goat
    Baby Goat Terrine, 139
    Baby Goat with Beets, Cinnamon-Clove Yogurt, and Charred Bread Emulsion, 136, 137–38
Gonçalves, Pedro, 50, 51
Grape Jam, Concord, 208
    Foie Gras Terrine with Concord Grape Jam and Charred Quince, 124–25, 127
Green Beans with Peaches and Almonds, 168
greens
    Caldo Verde (Collard Greens Soup), 13, 153
    Vinegared Kale Puree, 174
    See also broccoli raab
grilling, 130, 131
    Grilled Marinated Quail, 121, 122–23
    Grilled Sardines with Charred Peppers, 74, 75
    Marinated Grilled Pork Tenderloin, 86
Gutenbrunner, Kurt, 19

H
ham, 99
hazelnuts: Chocolate-Hazelnut Sauce, 209
herbs, 244
    Heirloom Tomato Salad with Black Olives and Herbs, 150, 151
    Herb Puree, 238
Parsley, Dill, or Basil Oil, 239
Herdade do Esporão, 141, 152
hot sauce: Piri Piri, 236

I
Iceberg, Cucumber, and Tomato Salad, 144

J
Jam, Concord Grape, 208
    Foie Gras Terrine with Concord Grape Jam and Charred Quince, 124–25, 127
jus
    duck jus, 108–9
    Pork, Beef, or Lamb Jus, 230

K
Kale Puree, Vinegared, 174
Koschina, Dieter, 145

L
La Bastide de Moustiers, 18

lamb
    Glazed Lamb Shoulder, 133
    Lamb Jus, 230
    Lamb Stock, 228
L'Arpège, 18, 168, 184
Leitão (Roast Suckling Pig), 88–89, 90, 91
Lespinasse, 18
Le Zoo, 18
Lime and Shiso, Sea Urchin Toasts with, 78, 79
linguiça. See sausage
Lisbon
    Cervejaria da Esquina, 56, 187
    Cervejaria Ramiro, 13, 50, 51, 99
    Pastéis de Belém, 211
Litchi, Salt Cod Confit with Coriander Dashi, Shiitake, and, 41
Lobster Stock, 232

M
Madeira, 223
Martina, Joao, 42–43
meat, 128–39
    See also beef; goat; lamb; pork; venison
Mexilhoeira Grande, 145
migas
    Cauliflower and Bacon Migas, 192, 193
    Roast Chicken Breasts with Bread Stuffing, 116
    Tomato, Bread, and Egg Stew, 154, 155
Mint, Fava Beans with Morcella and, 166, 167
morcella. See sausage
Moreira, Marco, 19
Mozambique Shrimp and Okra with Piri Piri, 52, 53
mushrooms
    Fried Eggs with Chanterelles, Morcella, and Potatoes, 104, 105
    Salt Cod Confit, Coriander Dashi, Shiitake, and Litchi, 41
    Shiitakes and Girolles with Wheat Berries, 184–85
    White Button Mushroom Stew, 182, 183
    Wild Mushrooms with Brussels Sprouts, 180
mussels
    Mussel Soup, 159–60, 161
    Seafood Rice, 56, 57

O
O Chico, 152, 166
octopus, 60
    Octopus and Black-Eyed Pea Salad, 62, 63
    Octopus Confit, 61
O Curral, 24
oil. See olive oil
okra: Mozambique Shrimp and Okra with Piri Piri, 52, 53

olive oil, 244, 245
    Garlic Oil, 241
    Olive Oil Cake, 220, 221
    Parsley, Dill, or Basil Oil, 239
    Potatoes in Olive Oil Confit, 195
olives
    Farm Egg, Salt Cod, Black Olives, and Crunchy Potatoes, 30, 31, 33
    Heirloom Tomato Salad with Black Olives and Herbs, 150, 151
Omelet, Linguiça, Chouriço, and Parsley, 102, 103
onions
    Refogado, 235
    Salt Cod with Smashed Potatoes and Spring Onions, 35
    Tuna, Tomato, and Onion Salad, 146, 147
    See also ramps
orzo: Chicken and Orzo Soup, 117–18, 119
Ourem, 24
Oxtail, Braised, 132

P
pantry ingredients, 244–45
paprika, smoked. See pimentón
parsley
    Herb Puree, 238
    Linguiça, Chouriço, and Parsley Omelet, 102, 103
    Parsley Oil, 239
Partridge Escabeche, 120
Passard, Alain, 18, 19, 168
Pastéis de Belém, 211
Pastéis de Nata (Crispy Egg Custard Tarts), 211, 212–13, 213
Peaches and Almonds, Green Beans with, 168
peas
    Eggs Baked with Peas, Linguiça, and Bacon, 100, 101
    Salt Cod with Ramps, Sweet Peas, and Linguiça, 40
    Spring Pea Soup, 158
    See also black-eyed peas
pepper, 244
peppers
    Grilled Sardines with Charred Peppers, 74, 75
    Piri Piri, 236
petiscos, 32
Pickles, 200–201
    Pork Belly and Clams with Pickles, 82–83, 85
Pigs' Ears, Crispy, with Ramps and Cumin Yogurt, 94, 95
Pig's Trotters Terrine, 92–93
pimentón, 244
    Piri Piri, 236
    Refogado, 235
    Tuna with Cucumber, Smoked Paprika, and Vinho Verde, 76, 77

Piri Piri, 236
  Mozambique Shrimp and Okra with Piri
    Piri, *52*, 53
Plums, Vinho Verde-Poached, 218
pork, 80–105
  about, 88–89, 99
  Braised Pork Belly, 97
  Crispy Pigs' Ears with Ramps and Cumin
    Yogurt, 94, *95*
  Cured Pork Loin, 87
  Marinated Grilled Pork Tenderloin, 86
  Pig's Trotters Terrine, 92–93
  Pork Belly and Clams with Pickles, 82–83,
    85
  Pork Jus, 230
  Pork Stock, 228
  Roasted Pork Belly, 96
  Roast Suckling Pig, *90*, *91*
  Spiced Pork Belly Cracklins, 98
  See also bacon; sausage
Porto, *58, 59, 60*, 223
  A Grade, 58–60, *59, 60*
Portuguese wines, 140–41, 223
  See also vinho verde
port wines, 223
  Port Caramel, 222
potatoes
  Farm Egg, Salt Cod, Black Olives, and
    Crunchy Potatoes, *30*, 31, *33*
  Fried Eggs with Chanterelles, Morcella, and
    Potatoes, *104*, 105
  Fried Shoestring Potatoes, 194
  Potatoes Confit, 195
  Salt Cod and Potato Croquettes, *25*, 28
  Salt Cod, Potato, and Egg Casserole, 36,
    37
  Salt Cod with Smashed Potatoes and
    Spring Onions, 35
  Warm Smashed Potatoes, 196, *197*
poultry, 106–27
  Grilled Marinated Quail, 121, *122–23*
  Partridge Escabeche, 120
  See also chicken; duck
pudding
  Cinnamon-Vanilla Rice Pudding, 217
  Corn Pudding, 216
pumpkin
  Pumpkin Fritters (Filhozes), 210
  Roasted Squash Soup, 157
puree
  Apricot Puree, 242
  Herb Puree, 238
  Vinegared Kale Puree, 174

Q

Quail, Grilled Marinated, 121, *122–23*
Quick-Fix Stock, 115

quince
  Brussels Sprouts with Quince and Bacon,
    176, *177*
  Foie Gras Terrine with Concord Grape Jam
    and Charred Quince, 124–25, *127*
  pickled, 200–201

R

ramps
  Crispy Pigs' Ears with Ramps and Cumin
    Yogurt, 94, **95**
  pickled, 200–201
  Salt Cod with Ramps, Sweet Peas, and
    Linguiça, 40
Red Snapper with Shellfish, Tomato, and Saf-
  fron (Caldeirada), 70–71, *72*
Refogado, 235
restaurants
  A Grade, 58–60, *59, 60*
  Aldea, 12–13, 17, 18–20, *21*, 32, 46
  author's restaurant background, 16–17,
    18–19
  Casa do Povo, 42–43
  Casa Vidal, 88–89, *89*
  Cervejaria da Esquina, 56, 187
  Cervejaria Ramiro, *13*, 50, *51*, 99
  O Chico, 152, 166
  O Curral, 24
  Seabra Marisqueria, 82
  Vila Joy and Vila Lisa, 145
rice, 186–87
  Cinnamon-Vanilla Rice Pudding, 217
  Duck Rice, 108–10, *111*
  Saffron Rice with Seared Shrimp and Foie
    Gras, 54–55
  Seafood Rice, 56, *57*
  Spring Chicken Rice, 114–15
  Tomato Rice, 186, 188, *189*
Ricotta Cream, Strawberries with, 219
Roquette, Antonio, 152

S

saffron
  Coconut-Saffron Cauliflower and Broccoli,
    171, *173*
  Mussel Soup, 159–60, *161*
  Red Snapper with Shellfish, Tomato, and
    Saffron (Caldeirada), 70–71, *72*
  Refogado, 235
  Saffron Rice with Seared Shrimp and Foie
    Gras, 54–55
salads, 144–51
  Heirloom Tomato Salad with Black Olives
    and Herbs, 150, *151*
  Iceberg, Cucumber, and Tomato Salad, 144
  Octopus and Black-Eyed Pea Salad, *62*, 63
  Salt Cod and Chickpea Salad, *38*, 39

Sardines with Spring Greens and Almonds,
  148, 149
  Tuna, Tomato, and Onion Salad, 146, *147*
Salami, Chocolate, 214
salt, 244
salt cod, 22–41
  about, 24
  Basic Salt Cod, 26–27
  Farm Egg, Salt Cod, Black Olives, and
    Crunchy Potatoes, *30*, 31, *33*
  Salt Cod and Chickpea Salad, *38*, 39
  Salt Cod and Potato Croquettes, *25*, 28
  Salt Cod Confit, Coriander Dashi, Shiitake,
    and Litchi, 41
  Salt Cod, Potato, and Egg Casserole, 36,
    37
  Salt Cod with Broccoli Raab, 34
  Salt Cod with Ramps, Sweet Peas, and
    Linguiça, 40
  Salt Cod with Smashed Potatoes and
    Spring Onions, 35
  soaking, 24, 26, 27
sardines, 60, 73
  Grilled Sardines with Charred Peppers,
    74, *75*
  Sardines with Spring Greens and Almonds,
    148, 149
sauces
  Apple-Watercress Sauce, Seared Scallops
    with, 69
  Caldeirada Sauce, 70–71
  Charred Bread Emulsion, 138
  Chocolate-Hazelnut Sauce, 209
  Coconut Sauce, Zucchini and Squash with,
    169
  Garlic Oil, 241
  Herb Puree, 238
  Parsley, Dill, or Basil Oil, 239
  Piri Piri, 236
  Pork, Beef, or Lamb Jus, 230
  Port Caramel, 222
  Salted Caramel Sauce, 205
  Shrimp Essence, 232
  Squid Ink Sauce, 237
sausage, 244
  Collard Greens Soup (Caldo Verde), 13,
    153
  Eggs Baked with Peas, Linguiça, and Bacon,
    100, 101
  Fava Beans with Morcella and Mint, 166,
    167
  Fried Eggs with Chanterelles, Morcella, and
    Potatoes, *104*, 105
  Linguiça, Chouriço, and Parsley Omelet,
    102, *103*
  Mussel Soup, 159–60, *161*
  Salt Cod with Ramps, Sweet Peas, and
    Linguiça, 40
scallops
  Seafood Rice, 56, *57*

Seared Scallops with Apple-Watercress Sauce, 69
Seabra Marisqueria, 82
seafood, 44–79
    about, 46, 50, 73
    Caldeirada (Red Snapper with Shellfish, Tomato, and Saffron), 70–71, *72*
    Clams Steamed with Vinho Verde, Garlic, and Cilantro, 64, *65*
    Goan Cuttlefish Coconut Curry, *66, 67–68*
    Lobster Stock, 232
    Mussel Soup, 159–60, *161*
    Octopus and Black-Eyed Pea Salad, *62, 63*
    Octopus Confit, 61
    Pork Belly and Clams with Pickles, 82–83, *85*
    Seafood Rice, 56, *57*
    Seared Scallops with Apple-Watercress Sauce, 69
    Sea Urchin Toasts with Shiso and Lime, 78, *79*
    Squid Ink Sauce, 237
    See also fish; salt cod; shrimp
sea urchins
    Seafood Rice, 56, *57*
    Sea Urchin Toasts with Shiso and Lime, 78, *79*
shallots, pickled, 200–201
shellfish. See seafood; specific types
shiitakes
    Salt Cod Confit with Coriander Dashi, Shiitakes, and Litchi, 41
    Shiitakes and Girolles with Wheat Berries, 184–85
Shiso and Lime, Sea Urchin Toasts with, 78, *79*
shrimp, 46, 50
    Garlic Seared Shrimp, 46, 48, *49*
    Mozambique Shrimp and Okra with Piri Piri, *52, 53*
    Saffron Rice with Seared Shrimp and Foie Gras, 54–55
    Seafood Rice, 56, *57*
    Shrimp Essence, 232
    Shrimp Stock, 232
Smoked Baby Beets, 178
smoked paprika. See pimentón
snacks
    petiscos, 32
    See also cracklins
Sonhos (Cinnamon-Sugar "Doughnuts"), 204, *207*
soups and stews, 153–63
    about, 152
    Cabbage and Tomato Soup, 156
    Chicken and Orzo Soup, *119*
    Collard Greens Soup (Caldo Verde), 13, 153
    Mussel Soup, 159–60, *161*

Red Snapper with Shellfish, Tomato, and Saffron (Caldeirada), 70–71, *72*
    Roasted Squash Soup, 157
    Spring Pea Soup, 158
    Tomato, Bread, and Egg Stew (Açorda), 154, *155*
    White Button Mushroom Stew, *182, 183*
    See also rice
sous-vide cooking
    Duck Rice, 108–10, *111*
    Glazed Lamb Shoulder, 133
    Partridge Escabeche, 120
    Red Snapper with Shellfish, Tomato, and Saffron (Caldeirada), 70–71, *72*
    Roasted Pork Belly, 96
Spanish ham, 99
Spice Mix, Goan, 233
Spring Chicken Rice, 114–15
Spring Greens and Almonds, Sardines with, *148*, 149
squash
    Pumpkin Fritters (Filhozes), 210
    Roasted Squash Soup, 157
    Zucchini and Squash with Coconut Sauce, 169
Squid Ink Sauce, 237
stews. See rice; soups and stews
stocks, 92
    Brown Chicken Stock, 227
    Chicken Stock, 226
    Coriander Dashi, 231
    Pork, Beef, or Lamb Stock, 228
    Quick-Fix Stock, 115
    Shrimp or Lobster Stock, 232
    Vegetable Stock, 226
    See also jus
Stonehenge Inn, 16
Strawberries with Ricotta Cream, 219
suckling pig, 88–89
    Roast Suckling Pig, *90, 91*

T

Tarts, Crispy Egg Custard (Pastéis de Nata), 211, 212–13, *213*
terrine
    Baby Goat Terrine, 139
    Foie Gras Terrine with Concord Grape Jam and Charred Quince, 124–25, *127*
    Pig's Trotters Terrine, 92–93
Toasts, Sea Urchin, with Shiso and Lime, 78, *79*
Tocqueville, 19, 20, 54
tomatoes
    Cabbage and Tomato Soup, 156
    Heirloom Tomato Salad with Black Olives and Herbs, 150, *151*
    Iceberg, Cucumber, and Tomato Salad, 144
    Red Snapper with Shellfish, Tomato, and Saffron (Caldeirada), 70–71, *72*

Tomato, Bread, and Egg Stew (Açorda), 154, *155*
Tomato Confit, 243
Tomato Rice, 186, 188, *189*
Tuna, Tomato, and Onion Salad, 146, *147*
tuna, 146
    Tuna, Tomato, and Onion Salad, 146, *147*
    Tuna with Cucumber, Smoked Paprika, and Vinho Verde, *76, 77*

V

Vaz Oliveira, Miguel, 152, 166
Vegetable Stock, 226
Venison in Juniper-Pepper Crust, 134, *135*
Vila Joy, 145
Vila Lisa, 145
Vinegared Kale Puree, 174
vinho verde, 140, 244
    Clams Steamed with Vinho Verde, Garlic, and Cilantro, 64, *65*
    Tuna with Cucumber, Smoked Paprika, and Vinho Verde, *76, 77*
    Vinho Verde–Poached Plums, 218

W

Wallsé, 19
watercress: Apple-Watercress Sauce, Seared Scallops with, 69
Wheat Berries, Shiitakes and Girolles with, 184–85
wild mushrooms
    Wild Mushrooms with Brussels Sprouts, 180
    See also mushrooms
wines, 140–41, 223
    See also vinho verde

Y

yogurt
    Baby Goat with Beets, Cinnamon-Clove Yogurt, and Charred Bread Emulsion, *136*, 137–38
    Crispy Pigs' Ears with Ramps and Cumin Yogurt, 94, *95*

Z

Zucchini and Squash with Coconut Sauce, 169

EDITORS
Leslie Stoker and Holly Dolce

DESIGNER
William van Roden

PRODUCTION MANAGER
Anet Sirna-Bruder

Library of Congress Control Number: 2014930936

ISBN: 978-1-61769-126-3

Copyright © 2014 by George Mendes and Genevieve Ko

All Photographs © 2014 by Romulo Yanes, except:

© Genevieve Ko: pp.2, 7, 10–11, 13, 22–23, 29, 43, 44–45, 51, 59, 60, 80–81, 89, 106–107, 126, 128–129, 131 (bottom), 141, 142–143, 162, 164–165, 172, 181 (top), 202–203, 213, 224–225, 246, 247, 249, 256

Courtesy of the Mendes family: pp.15, 47, 131 (top), 187

© Sofia Alves: pp.84, 206, 234

Published in 2014 by Stewart, Tabori & Chang, an imprint of ABRAMS. All rights reserved. No portion of this book may be reproduced, stored in a retrieval system, or transmitted in any form or by any means, mechanical, electronic, photocopying, recording, or otherwise, without written permission from the publisher.

Printed and bound in China
10 9 8 7 6 5 4 3 2 1

Stewart, Tabori & Chang books are available at special discounts when purchased in quantity for premiums and promotions as well as fundraising or educational use. Special editions can also be created to specification. For details, contact specialsales@abramsbooks.com or the address below.

ABRAMS
THE ART OF BOOKS SINCE 1949

115 West 18th Street
New York, NY 10011
www.abramsbooks.com

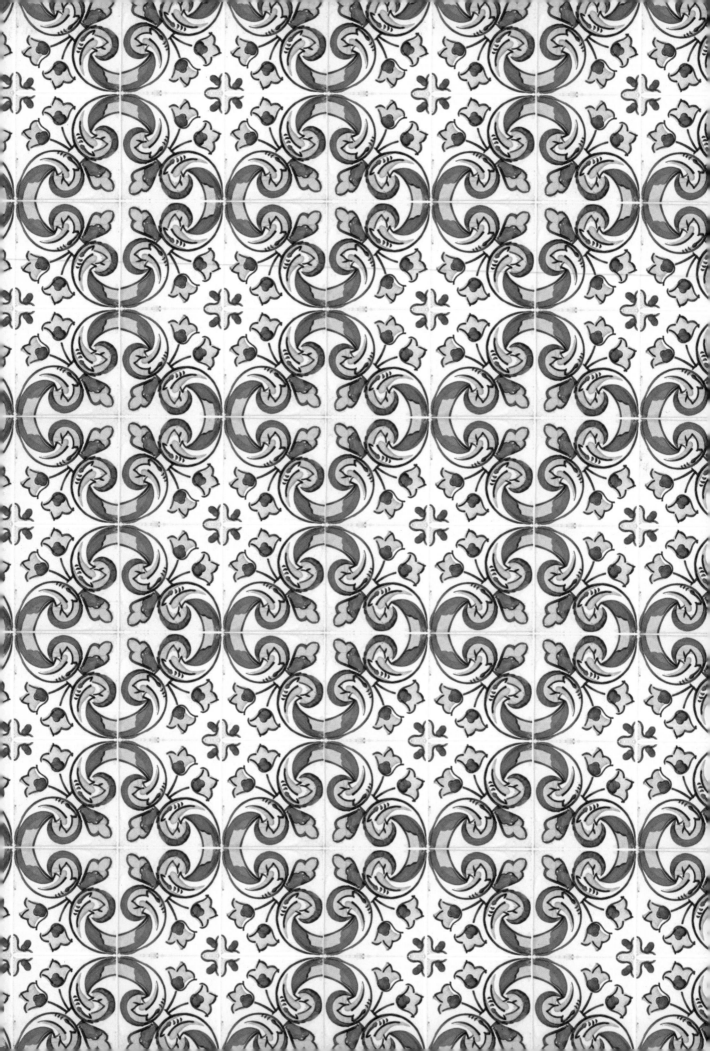